W9-BHG-450

Shelley's Study Guides

Herman Melville's MOBY DICK

A Study Guide

BY HANS GOTTSCHALK

EDITED BY WALTER HARDING

Shelley Publishing Company ★ Bound Brook, New Jersey

Library of Congress Number: 62–22299

Manufactured in the United States of America
by H. Wolff, New York
Designed by Robin Fox
Cover design by Charles Huck

Contents

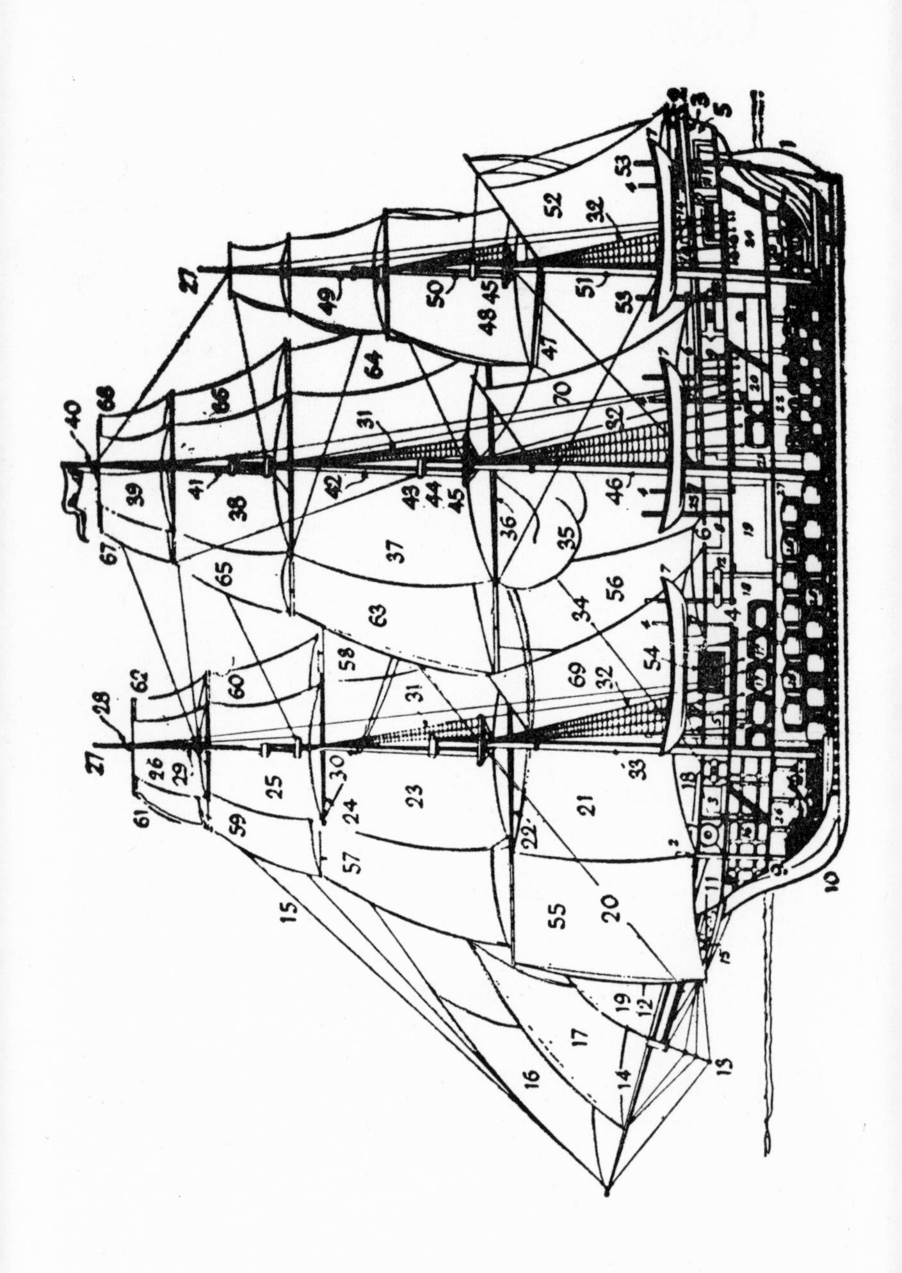

A WHALESHIP (Sectional Drawing)

LARGE NUMERALS

1. Rudder
2. Taffrail
3. Quarter-deck
4. Channels
5. Bulwarks
6. Waist
7. Hull
8. Keel
9. Bow
10. Stem
11. Hawse hole
12. Bowsprit
13. Martingale
14. Jib boom
15. Fore-royal stay
16. Flying jib
17. Standing, or outer, jib
18. Cathead
19. Fore-topmast staysail
20. Forestay
21. Foresail, or forecourse
22. Foreyard
23. Fore-topsail
24. Fore-topsail yard
25. Fore-topgallant sail
26. Fore-royal sail
27. Fore-truck, main-truck, mizzen-truck
28. Fore-royal mast
29. Fore-topgallant mast
30. Fore-topmast
31. Topmast shrouds
32. Lower shrouds
33. Foremast
34. Mainstay
35. Mainsail
36. Mainyard
37. Main-topsail
38. Main-topgallant sail
39. Main-royal
40. Main-royal-mast
41. Main-topgallant mast
42. Main-topmast
43. Main-mast cap
44. Main-mast-head
45. Maintop, mizzentop
46. Main-mast
47. Crossjack yard
48. Mizzen topsail
49. Mizzen topgallant mast
50. Mizzen topmast
51. Mizzenmast
52. Spanker
53. Davits
54. Try-works
55. Lower studding sail (stunsail)
56. Main studding sail
57. Fore-topmast studding sail
58. Lee fore-topmast studding sail
59. Fore-topgallant studding sail
60. Lee fore-topgallant studding sail
61. Fore-royal studding sail
62. Lee fore-royal studding sail
63. Main-topmast studding sail
64. Lee main-topmast studding sail
65. Main-topgallant studding sail
66. Lee main-topgallant studding sail
67. Main-royal studding sail
68. Lee main-royal studding sail
69. Fore spencer
70. Main spencer

SMALL NUMERALS

1. Windlass
2. Pawl-bitt
3. Forecastle companion
4. Boat-bearers
5. Fore hatch
6. Gallows for spare boats
7. Whaleboats
8. Main hatch
9. Booby hatch
10. Cabin skylight
11. Wheel
12. Hawse-chocks
13. Galley
14. After-house
15. Figure-head
16. Forecastle
17. Casks for oil
18. Fore 'tween decks
19. Blubber-room
20. Steerage
21. Chain-locker and pumps
22. After hold with stores, gear, etc.
23. Captain's stores
24. Captain's cabin
25. Boat-cranes
26. Fore hold with shooks, gear, etc.
27. Lower main hold
28. Casks for oil

Preface

This Guide is prepared to help students and others in the reading of *Moby-Dick,* not to do that reading for them. *Moby-Dick* was an exhilarating yet spiritually depleting book to write. Melville attempted the practically impossible, to catch cosmic metaphor in a single confine. Ought the reader then not be left to a parallel exhilarating of self-discovery, to experience and measure the impact of the book through achieving his own mastery of it? But what if the book is beyond him, temporarily, because it does not fly the form signals of the literary conventions to which he is accustomed? "Sink or swim" may lead to much more than uncomfortable moments.

The question guide proper proceeds chapter by chapter. There are no plot summaries as such, but from time to time there are recapitulations of themes, both within the questions and preceding groups of chapters. The questions themselves are designed to look beyond, to project to the probable future of men and events, as well as to understand the current through the recalled. Here and there appear research questions usable for background study, for essay questions, for oral reports, or for paper assignments. Allusions and terms for special checking appear at chapter ends.

Even a glance at the critical compendium indicates how a book as metaphorical as *Moby-Dick* necessarily prompts various overall interpretations. Generally the aim of the entire Guide is to suggest avenues of interpretation, not to pursue particular theories. These remain primarily in the province of research and criticism. See Chapter XCIII: The Castaway, page 51 for sample answers to questions.

For the map and the dictionary of sea terms I am indebted to Willard Thorp's edition of *Moby-Dick*. New York: Oxford University Press, Inc., 1947.

TABLE OF ORGANIZATION

I. Chapters 1—21: Ashore

Chapter 1: Manhattan

Chapters 2—13: New Bedford

Queequeg and Ishmael, from "Counterpane" to "Nighgown"

Chapel—Pulpit—Father Mapple's Sermon

Chapters 14—22: Nantucket

Preparations and Prophesies (Advent)

Weighing Anchor (Christmas)

II. Chapters 23—the end: At Sea

Chapters 23—47: Enroute to Whaling Grounds

People: Advocate, Knights and Squire, Ahab, Crew

Ship: Specksynder, Cabin Table, Mast-Head, Quarter Deck, Forecastle, The Chart, The Mat-Maker

Whales: Cetology, Moby-Dick, Whiteness of the Whale, Affidavit

Chapters 48—105:.The Broader Whaling Core (On Whaling Grounds)

Whales/Whaling/Whale Environment	*The Story/The Gams*
	48–54: 1st Lowering, Fedallah, Spirit Spout 1st Gam—*Albatross* 2nd Gam—*Town Ho*
55–59: Representations of Whales Whale Environment	
	61: Stubb Kills a Whale
60, 62–63: Line and Harpoon	
	64–5: Stubb Eats Whale
66–70: Exterior of Whale	
	71–73: 3rd Gam—*Jereboam* Monkey-Rope (Queequeg and Ishmael) Right Whale Killed
74–80: Head of Whale	
	81: 4th Gam—*Virgin*
82–90: Rest of Whale Whales in Natural Environment	

91: 5th Gam—*Rose-Bud*

92: Ambergris

93: Pip Overboard

94–98: Rendering the Whale

99–100: The Doubloon
6th Gam—*Samuel Enderby*

101–105: The Defleshed Whale
The Whale's Future

Chapter 105—the end: The Narrower Context of the Chase

The Remaining Gams: 7th—*Bachelor;* 8th—*Rachel*; 9th—*Delight*

Ahab's Preparations: Leg, Harpoon, Life-Buoy

The Pacific: Seductive, Raging, Just Right for both Combatants

Ahab and Starbuck: Ahab Gives In, Ahab With Musket, Starbuck With Musket, Ahab Confides—Starbuck Pleads

The Omens: Queequeg's Coffin, the Quadrant, the Corpusants The Needle, Log and Line, The Hat

The Chase on The Line: 1st, 2nd, 3rd Day (Death and Resurrection)

Herman Melville (1819-1891)

Melville's life and writings can be chronologically divided into four convenient periods. The first includes his youth on land; the second, his merchant marine, whaling and naval voyages; the third, the years of his creative peak; and the fourth, a long creative Autumn and Indian Summer.

I. Background and Youth on Land (1819-1839)

What antecedents led to the careers of seamanship and writing? Does young Ishmael parallel young Melville in any respects?

The sea was certainly in Melville's background. Both grandfathers were revolutionary heroes, military and naval. Father Allan Melville's import business necessitated trips abroad, of which he gave his family full and exciting accounts, by letter and in person. An uncle captained several merchantships. Cousins Guert Gansevoort, Peter Gansevoort, Thomas Wilson Melville Jr. took to sea, variously, on merchant, whaling and naval ships, and Melville had contact with them all. He himself made frequent short sailing trips during the New York years (1819-1830).

His education and apprenticeships were not, however, directed toward the sea. His schooling, both in New York and Albany, tended toward a dual curriculum—classical and commercial—and the Christian religious instructions heavily a part of all education at the time. The religious instructions and devotional contacts in his own family included Unitarian, Dutch Reformed, Presbyterian, Congregational, Episcopalian, and Catholic. Melville's religious background was not the strongly Calvinistic Presbyterian one of Ishmael.

The Melville family life, progressing geographically from a downtown boarding house to a nearly new house on the upper Broadway (No. 675) horsecar line, was a very warm, full, and stimulating one. And the immediate circle was extended by frequent visits to the Melvilles in Boston and Pittsfield and the Gansevoorts (mother Maria's family) in Albany.

Then the first of four financial reverses struck. The father entered bankruptcy in 1831, and then took a managership in the Albany branch of a New York fur concern. At the end of 1831 came a second financial reverse, one from which the father did not recover; his mind became deranged and he died a month later. The older boys had now to help with the providing. Gansevoort, brilliant Classical scholar, succeeded in commerce; Herman meanwhile successively tried clerking in a bank, farming and helping in the fur business. The latter was however wiped out by the Panic of 1837. The mother, mortgaging lots from her estate, had to follow Gansevoort into bankruptcy. Gansevoort himself fell critically ill.

Herman tried to bolster the family finances through teaching a country school; through taking a course in surveying and engineering, which netted no job; and through writing, two pieces published in a Lansingburgh paper. The financial situation of the family being now utterly desperate, Herman tried the sea, on the *St. Lawrence,* out of New York to Liverpool, June 4, 1839.

II. At Sea (1841-1844)

The subheading serves dually, literally to characterize the period of Melville's voyages as a seaman, and figuratively to suggest his at-sea-ness about a career.

The voyage to Liverpool brought him to what was probably the worst slum anywhere, the waterfront territory of that port. His descriptions of the conditions in *Redburn* (1849) are not exaggerated, unbearable though they may seem. They formed the second block of experiences with a broader society, the first being the ships' crews in which he served.

Finding the family in still worse financial circumstances on his return, he taught school once more (December 1839-May 1840), but the Greenbush school closed for financial reasons, leaving him owed much of his salary. He tried anew to gain employment, with no success. During the Christmas season (the *Pequod* sails on Christmas Day) he cast his lot with the small but newly built whaler, the *Acushnet.*

After 16 months aboard, he and Tobias Green (the Toby of *Typee*) deserted together at Nukehiva, Marquesas Islands, and sought out the Taipi valley Melville's cousin Thomas Melville had visited earlier. Making his escape from the natives, Melville reached Nukehiva again and shipped on the already mutiny-ridden *Lucy Ann.* Refusing to serve further on her when she reached Papeete in Tahiti, Melville and others were placed in stocks as punishment. After his release, he shipped on the whaler *Charles and Henry* November 2, 1842 until it docked at Hawaii, April 26, 1843. On these whalers he had acquired the experience and lore that led to *Moby-Dick.*

Melville worked briefly in a Honolulu store and saw the conflict between American Mission civilizations and a temporary occupation by French (Catholic) naval vessels. Here and in his other island-hopping he witnessed the pejorative effect of supposedly Christian civilization upon the happy, unregenerate life of the natives, which came to fictional expression in *Omoo* (1847) and reached the ripeness of devastating social criticism in *Mardi* (1849).

On August 17th Melville shipped on the US naval frigate *United States.* Here he had two unforgettable experiences: a literate group of companions, readers and writers, among the crew; and the discipline of a man-of-war. Both are turned to fine fictional account in *White-Jacket* (1850). He was discharged October 14, 1844 in Boston.

III. "On The Line"—Creative Peak (1844-1850)

The tales of his travels were so vivid that a number of family members and friends urged him to write them for publication. He obliged, and settled down to marriage (Elizabeth Shaw, daughter of Chief Justice Lemuel Shaw, an old Boston friend of the family) and to children (Malcolm 1849, Stanwix 1851, Elizabeth 1853, Frances 1855), as well as to the writing of seven novels in seven years, including the vast, yet concentrated, bulk of *Moby-Dick* (*Pierre,* 1852, in addition to those already mentioned, and many book reviews). This literary pace, coming hard upon the tough, as well as toughening, rigors of seaboard life, at least temporarily depleted his powers.

Contributory to the ebbing of creative power were readers' (and book buyers') disinterest in books unlike the romances they had come to expect, and the loss of the stock of his books in the Harper fire of December 1853. The economic pinch forced a remove to a farm near Pittsfield, Massachusetts, which brought the compensatory nearness of the Hawthornes for a short period. Melville, already highly impressed by Hawthorne the writer, found Hawthorne the man as great. And Hawthorne literally fired Melville to the greater, deeper *Moby-Dick* that he wished to write, yet despaired of writing.

IV. Last Literary Period (1853-1891)

With the novels *Israel Potter* (1855), *The Piazza Tales* ("Benito Cereno" among them, 1856), and *The Confidence Man* (1857), Melville all but stopped the writing of fiction. Instead he turned to poetry, beginning with his poems on the Civil War (*Battle-Pieces and Aspects of the War,* 1866, with an essay embodying the Lincoln view toward the South). A trip to the Holy Land in 1856-7 resulted in *Clarel* (1876), a philosophical poem. Two more small books of poems followed near the end of his life—*John Marr and Other Sailors* (1888) and *Timoleon* (1891). "Billy Budd," a prose masterpiece written near the end, was not published until 1924.

That publication date tells a story. After his early days as something of a literary lion (1848-1850) Melville fell into partial popular and critical eclipse. After his death, despite obituary eulogies and re-evaluations written by his friends and admirers, the decline of his literary reputation persisted, and he was not to be "revived" until his centenary in 1919, when his elevation came as a kind of compensatory canonization for the years of critical neglect.

The Making of *Moby-Dick*

In perhaps the greatest, certainly the most often quoted, letter of Melville (June 1851) he told Hawthorne that his life dated from his 25th year, he having had no prior development at all. This was 1844, the year of his leaving the sea and beginning his writing. Subsequently he wrote Hawthorne that he was constantly changing and growing: "As long as we have anything more to do, we have done nothing." That was just after *Moby-Dick*.

Before the momentous year, Melville had published only the two "Fragments from a Writing Desk." The augury of literary things to come lies only in their romanticism, their Shakespearean echoes, their plenitude of allusion. *Typee* and *Omoo* contained these characteristics, but added the essential of direct experience to the vicarious one of reading.

May 1850 brings the earliest reference to *Moby-Dick*. Melville acknowledges the encouragement of Richard Henry Dana in writing a whaling book. By June he is promising Bentley, his English publisher, the new book for fall. Then come two incomparably vital events for Melville, man and artist: he receives and reads Hawthorne's *Mosses from an Old Manse;* and shortly thereafter, as he is writing, or about to write, a review of it, he meets Hawthorne himself. Much as Whitman is fired by Emerson, so is Melville fired by Hawthorne.

There is no doubt of Melville's feeling at the very height of his powers. His six-hour writing day on top of his farm chores and his reading is evidence enough. He asks Hawthorne, "Can you send me about fifty fast-writing youths, with an easy style and not averse to polishing their labors? If you can, I wish you would, because since I have been here I have planned about that number of future works . . ."

What Hawthorne's writings give Melville regarding the highest integrity of the artist, personal association corroborates and extends. Thus Melville, under the power of exchanges on every kind of metaphysical subject with Hawthorne, evidently undertakes to rewrite the whaling romance. His hope for a fall completion goes by the boards; despite rigorous application, he does not finish until nearly a year later. What is happening?

First, the inner stir is tremendous; as though Melville is possessed by the book writing itself through him, as much as he is the artist shaping his work. His re-discovery of Shakespeare just before teems in his brain. He speaks of "taking a book off the brain," surely much as he strips the whale from living leviathan to giant fossil. The magnitude of the Ahabian-Ishmaelian challenge resounds in "But it is this *Being* of the matter; say *Me,* a *God,* a *Nature,* so soon you jump off from your stool and hang from the beam."

Second, the romance becomes the final book. It takes on added whale cargo from J. Ross Browne's *Etchings of a Whaling Cruise,* William Scoresby's *An Account of the Arctic Region,* Thomas Beale's *Natural History of the Spermwhale,* and Frederick A. Bennett's *A Whaling Voyage Round the Globe,* but with the carcasses rendered, transmuted, ("Transformed Utterly, a terrible beauty is born") into rarest metaphorical spermacetti, many of whose "particular subordinate allegories" become revealed to him only after being marked by others (Hawthorne and Mrs. Hawthorne, for example—Melville's letter of January 8, 1852). It becomes a "sounding" of the cosmic depths: "In me divine magnanimities are spontaneous and instantaneous—catch them while you can . . . I have written a wicked book, and feel spotless as a lamb." A source charged with personal association is also at hand: Owen Chase's account of the famous *Essex* disaster (which serves as climactic catastrophe in *Moby-Dick*), given Melville by Chase's son during a gam near the site (later Melville saw Captain Owen Chase himself aboard the *Acushnet*). Meanwhile, outside his window is Greylock, an ever present image of Moby-Dick, "a snow hill in the air."

Thus, finally, it becomes a novel of novels, that not merely stretches, but literally bursts, the existing form of fiction, to embody the adventure narrative, the philosophical essay, the naturalist's observation, the drama's scenes and soliloquies, the epics sweep and epitome of an age, the short story. It stands in reach of content and grasp of form with Hawthorne's fiction, Emerson's essays, Thoreau's *Walden,* and Whitman's "leaves"—unique, and uniquely American, monuments of the broader conception of literary transcendentalism.

Chapter Analysis

I. *Loomings*

This is the first of a number of chapters in which characteristics of the narrator, Ishmael, are cumulatively revealed. Since all events to follow are seen through his eyes, and his consciousness, the point of view between present telling and past happenings is also gradually established.

1. When does Ishmael take to the sea?
2. What do ordinary men, thinkers and artists alike see in the sea?
3. Why does Ishmael go to sea as an ordinary sailor?
4. Why did merchant sailor Ishmael this time go on a whaling voyage?
5. How does the title of the chapter fit the text?
6. Where does the tense shift from present to past and why?

Ishmael, Cato, circumambulation, metaphysical, Jove, Narcissus, Rockaway Beach, Ibis, Gabriel

II. *The carpet bag*

1. Why is shelter necessary for Ishmael?
2. How is the title related to this theme?

Nantucket, Leviathan, Euroclydon, Comorrah, Lazarus, Dives

III. *The Spouter-Inn*

Ishmael encounters the first of his shipmates, harpooner Queequeg. The next few chapters show their growing friendship.

1. What is the kind of impression Ishmael gets of the entry and public room of the Spouter-Inn?
2. What age-impression do you get of Ishmael in this chapter?
3. What is the landlord's attitude toward Ishmael's hesitancy in bedding with the unknown "harpooneer"? What purpose do you think it is meant to serve for you as reader?
4. How would you characterize Ishmael's dialogue in his long speech to the landlord regarding the "harpooneer" selling his head? How does it compare with the narrative style?
5. Why do you think he fancies the "harpooneer" as an African worshipping a Congo idol? Is this a general human thinking pattern? Explain.
6. What is the significance of Ishmael's remark, "Better sleep with a sober cannibal than a drunken Christian"?

IV. *The counterpane*

1. In view of his name, is it significant that Ishmael has a stepmother?
2. What other characteristics can you list up to now that Ishmael has revealed about himself, either directly or indirectly?
3. What is the difference between the recalled experience

and the fright of the previous night? Which is meant to strike the reader as the more terrifying?

4. Whose point of view do we get of Queequeg's dressing? Is this the viewpoint of the time of happening? Why or why not?

5. How is the chapter title made more general than in its immediate sense?

V. *Breakfast*

1. What does the narrator's comment regarding the landlord's joking add to our picture of him?

2. What does the whalemen's breakfast suggest about assurance in people?

VI. *The street*

1. What does the phrase about cannibals "many of whom yet carry on their bones unholy flesh" tell about Ishmael? his comments regarding the Vermonters and Green Mountaineers come down to go whaling? the phrase "had it not been for us whalemen"?

2. Why, do you think, Ishmael concludes his paean on New Bedford with a paragraph on its women?

bumpkin, dog-days, Harp-Seed, scoria

VII. *The chapel*

1. Are the dates of the chapel tablets of any significance to our story?

2. Why does he term the inscriptions "lines that seem to gnaw upon all Faith, and refuse resurrections to the beings who have placelessly perished without a grave"?

3. Why the interweaving of past and present tense in this and the previous chapter?

4. How is his last paragraph an answer of faith to those

mourners who "still refuse to be comforted for those who we nevertheless maintain are dwelling in unspeakable bliss"?

5. What does this chapter add to our accumulated evidence about Ishmael's background and character?

Elephanta

VIII. *The Pulpit*

1. What is the significance of Father Mapple pulling the ropeladder into the pulpit after himself?
2. Does the ending of the chapter add anything significant to our knowledge of Ishmael?

IX. *The sermon*

Father Mapple's retelling of the Jonah story as one whaleman to his fellows highlights the interrelationship of destiny or fate (God) and individual freedom of the will (Jonah) and its moral implications.

1. How would you characterize Ishmael's attitude toward Father Mapple?
2. To whom are we indebted for the setting of all our attitudes thus far?
3. For whom is the story of Jonah a lesson?
4. What is the basic sin of all men? In what does it consist?
5. What did Jonah seek to do after his basic sin?
6. In giving the Captain's side of Jonah's passage-booking what type of sinner is pointed up?
7. Could the paragraph beginning "like one who after" be called a "classic simile"? Why or why not? Interpret the phrase "drowning down to sleep."
8. Why is Jonah called "the God-fugitive"?
9. What does Father Mapple mean by saying that Jonah's answer to the mariners was "forced from Jonah by the hard hand of God that is upon him"?

10. Are the mariners as "unreluctant" in the Bible version as in this one?

11. Why was Jonah's repentance the right kind?

12. Did God wait for Jonah's repentance?

13. What was the second lesson, the one directed primarily at the Father Mapples? Is this analogous to the duty of the Captain in the Jonah story? Do you think Father Mapple's warning might be intended for all those who address others, including writers?

14. Do you expect this sermon to be of continued importance in the book? Why or why not?

canticle, kelpy, Sodom, parricide, benediction

X. *A bosom friend*

1. What is the import of Ishmael's characterizing Queequeg as "George Washington cannibalistically developed"? How does this notion go with the earlier "Better sleep with a sober cannibal than a drunken Christian"? What other sentences here actually make an advance over the latter? in what does the advance consist?

2. What does Ishmael mean by saying that Queequeg, "this soothing savage," had redeemed his heart?

3. What is the essential difference between Queequeg's and Ishmael's approaches to becoming "bosom friends"? Is it significant that in Queequeg's language this relationship is expressed as "henceforth we were married"?

4. What do the last two paragraphs add to our increasing knowledge of Ishmael? Has any of this been previously implied? Relate the very end to Queequeg's description of their relationship.

5. What might this meeting and friendship suggest about the importance of these two in the rest of the story? Does your answer get substantiation from the gradual spelling out of Ishmael's (the narrator's) character?

phrenologically, Socratic wisdom, dyspeptic

XI. *Nightgown*

1. Ishmael the narrator comments, "There is no quality in this world that is not what it is merely by contrast." Can you cite previous examples from the book? Can you square this notion with your own everyday experiences?

2. Test similarly by your own ordinary experience (1) "No man can ever feel his own identity aright except his eyes be closed"; and (2) "How elastic our stiff prejucices grow when once love comes to bend them."

3. What is the progression from "the counterpane" of Chapter IV to "the nightgown" of this chapter?

4. What does the last sentence suggest about the time of happening and the time of Ishmael's retelling? Have you noted this division before? Is it merely chronological—that is, Ishmael would not likely tell the story till the actuality were finished—or do you note any other qualities in Ishmael's telling that stem from such deferment?

confabulations, warming-pans

XII. *Biographical*

This chapter might have been called *Queequeg,* but instead it continues the use of objects, places and situations as chapter headings, avoiding persons.

1. Queequeg's island is not on any map. This is readily understandable, especially for those days. But what of what follows, "true places never are"? Has Ishmael been concerned previously with what is as related to what seems?

2. Queequeg's discovery that Christians could be both miserable and wicked, taken with Ishmael's discovery of the natural innocence and dignity of the cannibal Queequeg, may point to Melville's associating himself with the prevalent 18th and 19th century notion of the innate goodness of nat-

ural man. Consult your reference library for information regarding the concept.

cannibal, propensity, ignominy

XIII. *Wheelbarrow*

1. Does narrator Ishmael make his companionship with Queequeg a racial as well as religious one? Why the title?
2. What three great American whaling ports have been mentioned? To which were the two going? Why?
3. Why do you think Queequeg saved the "bumpkin" who had made fun of him? What are the religious implications?
4. What anticipation of the future does the aftermath include? Of what significance is this?

calabash, boobies, consecrate, intolerableness

XIV. *Nantucket*

1. Why does Ishmael give us such a detailed look at Nantucket and its seamen?
2. Here is one of Ishmael's first allusions to the whaling industry. What does Ishmael seem to think of it? How is this impression conveyed to us?

gameson wights, quohogs, mastodon, Alexander, terraqueous, privateers, chamois

XV. *Chowder*

1. What are the ominous signs Ishmael lists as having affected him? Do you think these are meant to be but idle fancy?
2. How is the account of the Try Pots an illustration of what was said generally about Nantucket in the previous chapter?
3. Does it strike you that the voyage itself is a long time

coming? Why, do you think, we get so many preliminaries, including even a recipe for clam chowder?

Tophet, chowder

XVI. *The ship*

This and the following chapters mark the advent of the Christmas start of the voyage. Symbolically, they serve as a kind of structural Advent to that start, including Queequeg's Ramadan, Elijah's prophecies and the preparation and well wishes for the success of the voyage.

1. What do the words and the allusions listed for the chapters thus far tell you about Ishmael?
2. What impression are we meant to get of the *Pequod?* Would one be able to tell that it is a whaler?
3. Captain Peleg gives us our first allusion to Captain Ahab; how does this allusion here serve both plot and expository ends?
4. Why do you think Ishmael has come to the conclusion that "all mortal greatness is but disease"?
5. Why do you suppose Ishmael goes into detail regarding the contradictions in Nantucket Quaker seamen?
6. Does Bildad parallel his scriptural counterpart?
7. What additional facts about Ishmael do we glean from his bargaining for his lay?
8. Through Peleg we get what kind of impression of Captain Ahab? What is the purpose of such advance exposition of character?
9. Ishmael deliberately invokes Ahab's biblical counterpart. Is he right about that other Ahab's character? Do you think the name *will* prove prophetic, as had been forecast by the old squaw? Why or why not?

Lent, Ramadan, Medes, Canterbury Cathedral, Becket, grotesqueness, Pottowottamie, anomalously, sanguinary, immutableness, Bildad and Pegleg (Bible)

XVII. *The Ramadan*

1. What satiric inclusion does Ishmael make in his opening remarks regarding religious tolerance?

2. How Presbyterian are Ishmael's remarks about fasting and hell? How do his thoughts about religious practicality here fit his earlier remarks about Nantucket Quakers?

XVIII. *His mark*

1. Does Ishmael's placing of Queequeg in the "First congregation of this whole worshipping world" confirm any earlier impression of his (Ishmael's) religious belief?

2. Does Peleg's description of what he thought of when the *Pequod* was dismasted off Japan parallel Ishmael's religious belief? What does it confirm about Captain Ahab?

Philistine, Belial

XIX. *The prophet*

1. What do we learn about Ahab from the "beggar-like stranger"? Do you think it significant that this is the first time a person is used as chapter title?

2. Why does narrator Ishmael here invoke "Mene, Mene, Tekel Upharsin" from the Book of Daniel (5.25-28, the original handwriting on the wall)?

3. Does the biblical Elijah seem to have any application here?

confluent, small-pox, ineffable heavens, humbug

XX. *All astir*

1. Why do you think Captain Bildad did all the purchasing of supplies?

2. A whaling ship carries "spare everything," almost, but——————.

3. Do you suppose Bildad's sister, Aunt Charity, is mentioned because she is going to play a vital part in the voyage?

4. Was Ishmael at all uneasy at this time?

5. How does Ishmael through all these chapters build our feelings about whales?

XXI. *Going abroad*

1. What did Elijah confirm for Ishmael?
2. When had Captain Ahab come aboard?

Copy of Watts, apotheosis

XXII. *Merry Christmas*

1. Is Christmas a significant time to start a voyage? Why or why not? For whom?

2. Of what importance is it that Bildad was singing hymns, Peleg swearing and kicking, and some of the crew singing "profane songs"?

3. Are the lengthy, somewhat heavy-hearted farewells related at all to the items in question?

4. What does Ishmael mean in saying "we . . . blindly plunged like fate into the lone Atlantic."

XXIII. *The lee shore*

Here begins the second and greater structural division by locale—ashore and asea. The first section of the latter comprises the chapters (XXIII-XLVII) before the whaling grounds proper, the Season-on-the-Line, are reached, and thus permit a detailing of the ship's company, as a microcosm of life, including the helmsman, the narrator ("The Advocate"), the knights and squires (mates and harpooners), the captain, and the melting-pot crew.

1. What is the irony of a lee shore?

2. How does Ishmael apply this irony to Bulkington and, really, to all men? Could the application include writer and reader too?

3. Why should Ishmael include this single chapter as Bulkington's epitaph?

XXIV. *The advocate*

1. Who is the advocate here of the whaling industry? Why can he so readily say "us whalemen"?

2. Do you think whaling was as dangerous as war in the early 1800's?

3. How did whaling compare in importance with other industries of the time (research question)?

4. How could the whale-ship be termed a pioneer?

5. Test Ishmael's notion that whalemen were responsible for democracy in Peru, Chile and Bolivia and for the settlement of Australia.

6. What about the charges that whaling has no famous authors, no good blood, no respectability, no dignity?

defilements, carrion, apparition, puissant, cosmopolite

XXV. *Postscript*

1. In what way does this chapter lead to the title of the next, "Knights and Squires"?

XXVI. *Knights and squires*

1. List all the general characteristics attributed to Starbuck by narrator Ishmael.

2. What kind of bravery did Starbuck possess? What kind did he not have?

3. What does Ishmael think of mankind in general? Why?

4. Why, do you think, Ishmael feels that an absolute God makes true democracy possible among men?

5. Ishmael the narrator appeals to that God, that "Spirit of Equality," for help in telling his story. Why should he allude to Bunyan, Cervantes and Jackson?

The general answer is here. For reasons behind the three specific allusions consult an encyclopedia.

vicissitudes, intrepid

XXVII. *Knights and squires*

1. Why should this and the previous chapter be entitled "Knights and Squires"? Is this an allusion to literature as well as to life?

2. In epic poems of the classic type from Homer to Virgil down to the present, there are certain standard characteristics (1) appeal to the Muse; (2) listing and delineating the champions on both sides of the central conflict. These chapters seem to comprise such a listing of one side. What do you think the other side might be?

3. Distinguish among the temperaments of Stubb, Flask, and Starbuck.

4. Why would Melville select a South Sea Islander, an Indian, and an African negro to be his harpooners? Do the harpooners parallel their respective mates?

5. Would such terms as "melting pot," "international," "microcosm" and "frontier" have any application to the *Pequod* and her company?

impious, circumvention, Ahasuerus, residue

XXVIII. *Ahab*

Thus far the only chapter titles of persons have been "The Prophet," "The Advocate," and "Knights and Squires." This is the first chapter to bear a proper name as title.

1. Why does Ishmael call whaling a "Scandinavian vocation"?

2. What do knights and squires imply as overlord? Why is Ahab not designated so?

3. Why do you think Ishmael speaks of a crucifixion in Ahab's face?

4. List all the attributes that have thus far been applied to Ahab by various hands. What kind of impression do you get of Ahab from them? Keep your answers to hand for checking against Ahab's revealing himself in his words and actions.

livid, sepulchral, misanthropic

XXIX. *Enter Ahab; to him, Stubb*

The book continually relates interior and exterior life. Sometimes exterior action and reaction of the moment lead to interior rumination, as the exchange in this chapter leads to the reflections of Ahab and Stubb in the following two chapters.

1. Is there anything in the nature of the chapter which seems to demand its kind of title?

2. Why do you think Ahab dressed down Stubb so mercilessly?

deprecating

XXX. *The pipe*

1. How can Ishmael overhear Ahab here? Does this fact have anything to do with the questions just above?

2. Why does Ahab throw away his pipe?

XXXI. *Queen Mab*

1. Why would Stubb tell Flask about his dream?

2. That which bothers us most in our waking life tends to bother us most in our dreaming life, and so Stubb dreams of

Ahab's insulting and especially kicking him. Dreams are often distortions, inversions, recompositions of the real thing. Why does Stubb in his dream kick a pyramid instead of Ahab? How does the pyramid represent, or stand for, Ahab (Think also of the stance of Ahab at his quarter deck post)?

3. Whom does the merman represent? Why is he able to persuade Stubb to leave Ahab alone?

4. Why is the merman of the dream a hunchback? Why are there marlin spikes in his posterior when Stubb wants to kick him?

5. The allusion of the Chapter title is to Mercurio's Queen Mab speech in Shakespeare's *Romeo and Juliet.* Why is it invoked here?

merman, marlin spike

XXXII. *Cetology*

Melville ostensibly writes a novel yet utilizes dramatic techniques, as we have just seen, as well as epic ones. As in most epics, we get here a catalogue of the leaders of both sides (Greek and Trojans in *The Iliad,* angels and devils in *Paradise Lost*): men and whales, climaxed with the presentation of their respective champions, Ahab and Moby-Dick. It may be noted that unlike characteristic epics which begin *in medias res,* in the midst of the action, and return to the starting point via flashback, this book recounts its events chronologically.

1. Ishmael says that the whale needs documented categorization, and that he will lay down a plan therefor. To what field does such classification belong? Do you think Melville knew that?

2. Why does Ishmael remind us "But I have swam through libraries and sailed through oceans"?

3. Of what significance is it for his classification that Ishmael at the outset goes against Linnaeus and calls the whale a fish?

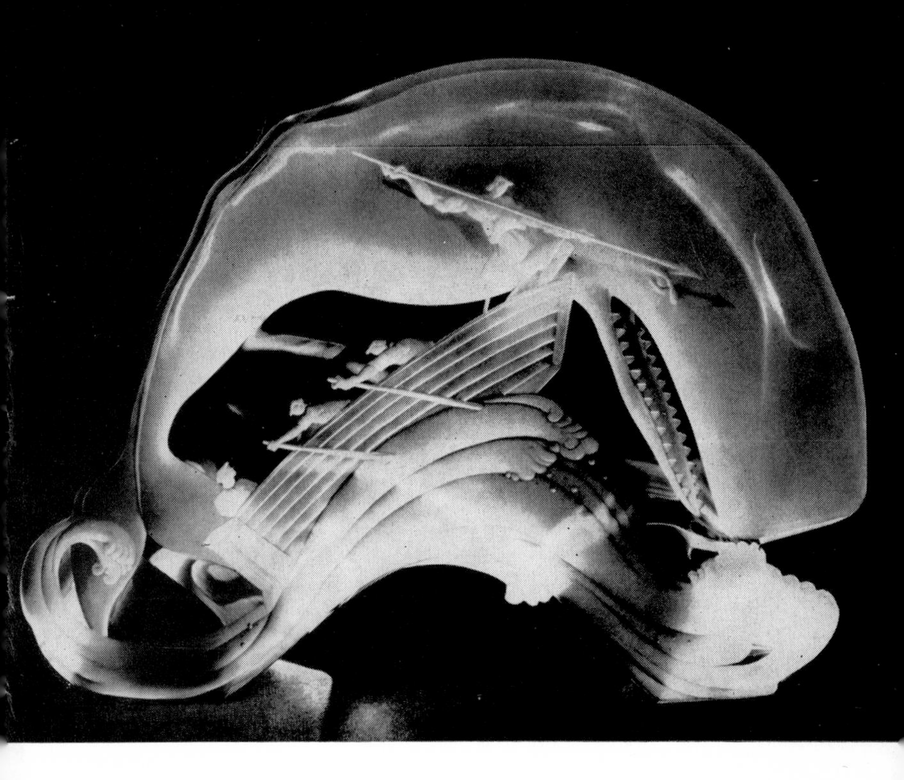

MOBY DICK

Glass design by Donald Pollard
Engraving design by Sidney Waugh
Height 8″ • Length 11¼″

Crystal form cut in the silhouette of the leaping whale engraved as a shadowy mass on its far side. In the foreground, the thickness of the crystal giving an illusion of intervening space, is engraved a rowboat. Its oarsmen pull against a heaving sea. At its prow stands a one-legged man about to hurl his lance into the whale.

The piece is an interpretation of the mortal struggle between Captain Ahab and the white whale, from Herman Melville's novel, *Moby Dick.*

Sidney Waugh, American sculptor, has designed the engraving for a great number of important Steuben pieces. Among these are the Zodiac Bowl, collection of The Metropolitan Museum of Art, and the Merry-Go-Round Bowl, collection of Queen Elizabeth II.

4. If the division of whales into books and chapters is not primarily one of science, of what field is it?

5. Note the specific descriptions of Book I (Folio) Chapter III (Fin-Back) which are not denotative, scientific information. What do these describe? In what terms? Is Ishmael developing any parallels between whales and men who catch them?

6. List key sentences that characterize the other species from the human point of view.

7. Melville's first draft of the book was an action story of whaling without such chapters as this. Why do you think he included them at all as part of a novel?

cetology

XXXIII. *The specksynder*

Thus far two major elements have been introduced: men and whales. Now we get a third: the positions and functions on shipboard, which are the means of meeting between the first two (here specksynder, cabin table, masthead, quarterdeck and forecastle). These three elements are interwoven and extended throughout the book.

1. Is the last paragraph of the previous chapter meant to provide any transition back to Ishmael's consideration of the men?

2. How is Ahab's "irresistible dictatorship" made possible by the ship's organization? What only does he demand of his men? What evidence have we had of this?

3. To what group of dictators is Ahab already forecast as belonging? What does this add to our picture of Ahab?

XXXIV. *The cabin-table*

1. Why do you suppose oriental titles of royalty are used here for the ship's officers (remembering that earlier they were knights and squires)?

2. What is added to our knowledge of Ahab by the concluding paragraph? Do you think Ishmael includes the sentence regarding Ahab's religion because it will prove important later?

emir, Belshazzar

XXXV. *The mast-head*

This chapter represents another way of relating inner and outer life—the merging of one into the other in a state of suspended action.

1. In his historical survey of mastheads Ishmael includes many land based ones. Why do you think he wishes to make a concept of masthead so much more inclusive?

2. The masthead, says Ishmael, "to a dreamy meditative man is delightful." Does he include himself among such? How is this description related to the peroration of Father Mapple's sermon (end of Chapter IX)?

3. Compare Melville's suggestion that the watchcoat (and other clothing) is merely an extension of the skin, though also something like a house, to the clothing-shelter philosophy of Thoreau in the first chapter of *Walden* and Carlyle in his *Sartor Resartus.*

4. What do the following phrases Ishmael uses of himself add to our mental picture of him: "lad with a lean brow and hollow eye"; "given to unseasonable meditativeness"; "with the Phaedon instead of Bowditch in his head"; "this sunken-eyed young Platonist"?

5. The ending seems to be a warning by Ishmael against becoming too involved, too subjective, and so losing detachment, distance, objectivity. Does this add a characteristic to our idea of him? List in review all the facts, characteristics and basic attitudes that have been used by Ishmael to characterize himself.

Babel, Admiral Nelson, Obed Macy, Cranmer, Pantheistic, Decartian vortices

XXXVI. *The quarter-deck*

1. What is the "one unsleeping, ever-paring thought" of Ahab that Ishmael refers to? Also, "the same intense bigotry of purpose in his aspect"?

2. What is unusual in Ahab's summoning all hands aft?

3. How do you account for Ahab's magnetic arousal of enthusiasm in the men here?

4. Compared to the lays for which the men were shipping, is the 16 dollar goldpiece a substantial incentive?

5. Have they really shipped to chase Moby-Dick? What is the significance of Ahab vowing to chase Moby-Dick even "round perdition's flames," and then saying "God bless ye, men" to their support of his purpose?

6. Are Starbuck's "long face" and holding back evidence of his mercenary nature?

7. In Ahab's explanation to Starbuck's charge of blasphemy for vengeance on "a dumb thing" what are the key words?

8. Even in this answer Ahab blasphemes. In what does his blasphemy consist?

9. Why does Ahab feel he has conquered Starbuck ("now is mine")?

10. What is the importance of Starbuck's murmured prayer "God keep me—keep us all!"?

11. What omens of unsuccess appear? Why only momentarily? What does the analogy of the wolf pack add?

12. Why does Ahab speak of the pope and his cardinals as cupbearers to "my three pagan kinsmen"? What ceremony is alluded to when he speaks of "the murderous chalices"? How would you characterize Ahab's spiritual nature here?

13. What does Ahab mean when he says "I do not order ye; ye will it"?

Leyden jar

XXXVII. *Sunset*

1. Why does Ahab say his crown is iron and that his "fixed purpose is laid with iron rails"? And why does he include "Over unsounded gorges, through the rifled hearts of mountains," and "under torrents' beds" in the territory of that purpose? Since behind Ahab is the mind of Ishmael and behind him the mind of Melville, what is this book beyond the story of men hunting whales, and even Ahab hunting down the white whale that incapacitated him?

3. Why does Ahab challenge the gods? Why does he call himself demoniac?

4. What do the following words suggest regarding Ahab's feeling of personal responsibility—"What I've dared, I've willed; and what I've willed, I'll do!"?

XXXVIII. *Dusk*

1. Does Starbuck's soliloquy or interior monologue tell anything about his feeling of personal responsibility? Does this have anything in common with Ahab's?

2. What does Starbuck mean by saying Ahab wants to be a democrat to all above yet a tyrant to all below?

3. How would you characterize Starbuck's spiritual nature?

demigorgon

XXXIX. *The first night-watch*

1. What is Stubb's attitude toward personal responsibility? Is it the same as that of Ahab and Starbuck?

2. In reviewing these three attitudes, what relationship do you find between personal responsibility and personal freedom or freedom of the will?

3. What has this second look at knights and squires added to the earlier one?

4. How are the three soliloquies just given examples of relating inner and outer life?

XL. *Midnight, forecastle*

1. Why are the men seemingly more affected by Ahab's wine than he and his officers?
2. What generalization do you draw from the identification of the various crewmen?
3. Why are there allusions to Christ, Brahma and Seeva?
4. What is the significance of Tashtego's remark about the dancing?
5. How are the rising wind, dark and lightning in nature paralleled among the men?
6. Why should it be the Spanish sailor who taunts Daggoo with his blackness?
7. What is the function of the Old Manx Sailor's comments?
8. Why does Pip think God is white?
9. Pip calls Ahab "that anaconda of an old man." Begin collecting the various animal metaphors and analogies applied to Ahab. Which have we had thus far?
10. What is the significance of the times of day for the quarterdeck ritual and the subsequent chapters?

XLI. *Moby-Dick*

Except for mythical Queen Mab (not a character here), "Moby-Dick" and "Ahab" are the only proper names to serve as chapter titles.

1. Of what importance is it that Ishmael reveals the part he had in the quarter deck ceremony staged by Ahab? Review also the motivation of the various men to this voyage.
2. Here is introduced the title character. Have we had any

conditioning regarding our attitude toward him? List the characteristics that have thus far been applied to him by various hands.

3. What in general was the factual record of Moby-Dick's exploits? Did rumor add to or subtract from these? We have here an illustration of how reality becomes myth. Cite several parallel extensions, non-human and human.

4. In the paragraph beginning "But there were still other . . ." what does the phrase "Not even at the present day" confirm about the novel's point of view?

5. The superstition of "groves of spears" in Moby-Dick and his high pyramidical white hump recall what in the Queen Mab chapter (XXXI)? What is the parallel? How do these parallel elements of Stubb's dream?

6. Does Ishmael want us to share the general belief that Moby-Dick manifested an "intelligent malignity"?

7. What qualities were inherent in Ahab's earlier assault on Moby-Dick? Do these qualities or characteristics seem to be still part of Ahab's make-up? Illustrate.

8. What does Ahab identify with Moby-Dick? Is your answer to question 7 pertinent here?

9. Of what importance is the fact that Ahab had to be straightjacketed in his hammock for the trip home after his encounter with Moby-Dick?

10. Why is it important that Ahab himself recognized "all my means are sane, my motive and my object mad"?

11. Ishmael here states Ahab's voyage purpose as "audacious, immitigable, and supernatural revenge" of an "ungodly old man." Cite the evidence previously manifested for this opinion.

12. The ship's crew "seemed specially picked and packed by some infernal fatality" to help Ahab to his revenge. This is one of a whole series of similar intimations by Ishmael. Is there a parallel fatality in Father Mapple's parable of the Jonah story?

13. In the last paragraph, what does the change in tense

from "to dive deeper than Ishmael can go" to "I . . . could see naught in that brute but the deadliest ill" imply?

Cuvier, Ophites, Hotel de Cluny, Thermes, Caryatid

XLII. *The whiteness of the whale*

1. How does the "at times" of the opening sentence modify your answer to the previous question?

2. What does Ishmael's expressions "the Romish faith" and "the Romish mass" say about his religion?

3. In his attribution of terror to white things (including Moby-Dick), in his feeling of "secrets which took hold of God" in the plumage of the albatross, Ishmael seems to parallel Ahab's attribution of malignity to Moby-Dick. Is there any difference? What is Ishmael getting at regarding the nature of Nature?

4. In the last chapter we suggested how reality extends into myth. Are the symbolizations of whiteness here enumerated extensions? How does your answer relate to your answer to question 4?

5. Ishmael says the whiteness in Nature preceded that in man's symbolization. He also says imagination is necessary for the experience of the latter. Do the qualities of terror, innocence, deathlikeness thus exist only in the mind?

6. What, then, does Ishmael mean when he characterizes whiteness as "at once the most meaning symbol of spiritual things, nay the very veil of the Christian's Deity; and yet should be as it is, the intensifying agent in things the most appalling to mankind"? Does this help answer how his and Ahab's notion compare?

Pegu, magniloquent, circumambient

XLIII. *Hark!*

1. Is this suggestion of somebody else on board the first such?

scuttlebutt

XLIV. *The chart*

1. Do you think Ahab's wrinkled forehead is meant as a parallel to that of Moby-Dick, as the parallel is made between Ahab's forehead and the lined charts which trace Moby-Dick's appearances?

2. In Father Mapple's sermon God prepared the whale for Jonah; here Ahab scientifically prepares to reach the whale. Does God enter into the latter at all, according to Ishmael?

3. What is Ahab's "hell in himself"? How does his monomaniac purpose make him schizophrenic?

4. How did Ahab in himself represent the parallel of the whale's whiteness?

5. How does the chart continue the third element, the means of meeting between whales and men, generally and specifically?

Mufti

XLV. *The affidavit*

1. Why does Ishmael invoke the classic names of Cambyses, Marius and Sylla when he lists four of the outstanding whales of whaling history?

2. Why is Ishmael at pains to prove that Moby-Dick is not "a monstrous fable, or still worse and more detestable, a hideous and intolerable allegory"?

3. There are naturally both tractable and mad whales as there are both kinds of dogs and cats. How does this fact fit Ishmael's and Ahab's attitude toward Moby-Dick?

4. Look up the circumstances of Melville meeting Owen Chase's son to see whether they are pertinent to the novel. Investigate also Ishmael's saying he is a nephew of Captain D'Wolf as it applies to author Melville.

5. How does the *affidavit* parallel the earlier *advocate?*

XLVI. *Surmises*

1. Why was Ahab concerned most with keeping Starbuck in line?

2. What did Ahab want to keep hidden from the crew?

3. What material purpose of the voyage does Ahab intend to maintain to control the crew?

4. Climactically, Ahab's last caution lay in what realization regarding his crew? What responsibility does this legal and moral aspect place upon the crew, as compared to that placed on Ahab as Captain?

XLVII. *The mat-maker*

Ishmael has twice referred to himself as a Platonist, that is, an idealist. For such a person nature is the symbol of spirit, as Emerson puts it. Therefore, as does Emerson and even more specifically Thoreau, Ishmael sees the idea which underlies all natural phenomena including also whales, water and sea-weed. As their spiritual part ever transcends their material one, it follows that all nature, the entire universe, is essentially spiritual and manifests the purposefulness of its Creator.

1. How does this chapter show Ishmael to be a transcendentalist with a small "t"?

2. Describe how in the metaphor of matmaking ("The Loom of Time") are interblended necessity or fate, individual liberty in freedom of the will, and chance.

3. Why should this metaphor be followed in the same chapter by the first sighting of the whale and by the appearance of Ahab's phantom crew?

samphire baskets

XLVIII. *The first lowering*

Approximately here begins the 2nd great section of division two—asea: It includes roughly chapters 48-105. Here is the true concentration on cetology and whaling in their actual and transcendental implications. Only a small number of chapters, devoted primarily to the symbolically significant gams, carry the quest for Moby-Dick forward.

1. How is Ahab's boat crew characterized spiritually? Does this equate at all with what Ishmael has told us of Ahab?

2. How is Ishmael's description of Ahab's words to his crew in character?

3. How are necessity, free will and chance interwoven in the adventure and rescue of Starbuck's boat (with Ishmael on his first lowering)?

enigmatical, binnacle compasses

XLIX. *The hyena*

1. Describe in your own words the kind of mood Ishmael here has in mind? Can you cite parallels? How does this relate to his sense of humor about things, including himself?

L. *Ahab's boat and crew. Fedallah*

1. Should Ahab have entered the small boat to chase whales? How does this relate to his knowledge regarding ship law and morality at the end of Chapter XLVI?

2. Here is the first hint of Fedallah's influence over Ahab. Is he human or not? Consult the Bible, Kings 22: 19-22.

LI. *The spirit-spout*

1. Why is it important that Fedallah first saw the spout? In its recurrence do you think it is in any way meant as an allusion to the pillar of fire which guided the children of Israel through the waterless wilderness?

LII. *The albatross*

1. What seemed, at least to superstitious sailors, two omens against hunting the White Whale? How are such omens both warnings and urgings to Ahab in his quest?

2. Omens or not, how does Ishmael at the close of the chapter prophesy the result of that quest?

fullers, raiment, Cyclades

LIII. *The gam*

This is the first of a series of gams. These are natural to a whaling voyage, but they are also structurally functional in the rest of the story, each making its own symbolic contribution to the literary voyage.

1. What is the essential nature of the gam? Why is it so vital among whalers?

2. Why, according to Ishmael, do other ships and companies look down on whalers and whalemen? Can you think of a more subtly psychological reason for their doing so?

3. What is Noah Webster's ark? Why does Ishmael use that pun?

descrying, provincialism, finical, lexicon

LIV. *The Town-Ho's story*

1. Now that the *Pequod* is southeast of the Cape of Good Hope, find its whereabouts on the map.

2. How did Ishmael have access to that part of the *Town-Ho's* story that Ahab and his officers and even the *Town-Ho's* captain did not know?

3. Ishmael narrates the story as a reproduction of his oral telling. This is the first time we get him in dialogue since his conversation with Elijah (Chapter XXI). Are these two instances and Ishmael's harangue of the Spouter-Inn landlord stylistically similar?

4. Why does Ishmael develop the whole analogy of the Great Lakes region as parallel to the ocean, say the Atlantic, and its land environs? Is it really necessary for the plot of the *Town-Ho* story?

5. What does Ishmael mean by calling Rodney "the predestinated mate" and saying "the fool had been branded for the slaughter by the gods"?

6. Do the analogies between the Erie and Venetian canals and corruption in canal cities, St. Marks and Lima ("The World's one Lima") square with your answer to question 4?

7. Why is Ishmael at such pains to have his story declared true?

8. What does this gam and its story add to the projected quest for Moby-Dick? Is it important that the crew only are in the know?

brig, Borean, maledictions, poniard, Ashantee, brigandish Canallers, miscreants, perfidious, archiepiscopacy

LV. *Of the monstrous pictures of whales*

1. Why does the concern regarding pictures of whales follow the *Town-Ho* story?

2. Is there a parallel between drawn and worded pictures of whales, whether true or false?

Vishnu, Matse Avator, Guido, Perseus, Andromeda, Hogarth, howdah vignettes, Saratoga, Baden-Baden, *Advancement of Learning,* veracious, heinousness, hippogriff, Richard III whales

LVI. *Of the less erroneous pictures of whales, and the true pictures of whaling scenes*

1. Why is Ishmael so concerned about artists getting action as well as fact into their pictures?

Pliny, Hackluyt, Patagonian, centaurs, tantamount, grapnel

LVII. *Of whale in paint; in teeth; in wood; in sheet-iron; in stone; in mountains; in stars*

1. What does Ishmael mean when he says all true whale-hunters are savage and that he owes "no allegiance but to the King of the Cannibals?"

2. Why does Ishmael call Greek sculptures and Albrecht Dürer savages?

skrim-shaw, Agro-navis, Cetus, Hydrus, fasces

LVIII. *Brit*

1. This chapter opens with still another analogy, that of seas of brit like fields of golden wheat. If we say that common to both is the idea of harvest-fieldness, what do we mean?

2. Try to get at the same kind of common element for the following analogies:
   (1) right whales eating brit like mowers cutting grain
   (2) black right whales seen from mastheads like black rock forms or (3) like recumbent Indian elephants

3. Does not today's conquest of the seas by man belie Ishmael's contention that "forever and forever, to the crack of doom, the sea will insult and murder him, and pulverize the stateliest, stiffest frigate he can make"?

4. What final analogy does Ishmael lead up to? What does it mean? Can you cite illustrations?

5. How can we perhaps say that the 2nd of the three major elements—the whale—has now been extended to include all sea-life and the very sea itself?

Crozetts, Korah, Tahiti

LIX. *Squid*

1. To the terror of the white spirit spout and white whale is added that of the great white squid. What kind of omen was it for sperm whalemen?

2. The battle lines are now clear: landbased puny men of intelligence and utter courage in fragile ships pitted against superlative brute whales in their natural sea-environment. How does this apply specifically to Ahab's quest?

Java, Kraken, cuttle-fish, Anak

LX. *The line*

Narrator Ishmael continues the interweaving of the three major elements, turning now once more to the positions and functions on shipboard, exploring each in both its actuality and transcendence.

1. How can it be said that literally the lives of six men hang on this line?
2. Why should there be so much joking in whale boats? Can you cite parallels?
3. How, would you say, are all men "enveloped in whale lines," "born with halters round their necks"?

hemp, Circassian, Mazeppa

LXI. *Stubb kills a whale*

1. What does Ishmael mean by "in that dreamy mood losing all consciousness, at last my soul went out of my body"? Compare Chapter XXXV.
2. What are the dangers of killing a whale?

luff, helm down, galliot

LXII. *The dart*

1. Out of his experience Ishmael suggests a change in the whaleboat. How does he mean the generalization he draws at the end of the chapter? How can it apply to literary harpooner Ishmael and author Melville?

LXIII. *The crotch*

1. How are necessity, chance, and free will manifested in the handling of the second iron in the crotch?

2. Earlier Ishmael spoke of chance as playing the largest role of the three in the affairs of men. Is this so for the harpooning of whales? Demonstrate.

LXIV. *Stubb's supper*

1. Why should sharks banqueting on dead whale lead Ishmael to say "If you have never seen that sight, then suspend your decision about the propriety of devil-worship, and the expediency of conciliating evil"?

2. Is Ishmael's remark regarding sharks following slave ships at all related to Stubb's ordering Fleece the cook to preach to the sharks?

3. Do you think Ishmael agrees with Fleece that "all angel is not'ing more dan de shark well governed"? Is this meant as applicable to Stubb?

4. What is the chapter meant to add to the revelation of Stubb's character?

epicurean

LXV. *The whale as a dish*

Several chapters now extend the second major element—the whale—intensively, into its make-up in both actual and transcendental terms.

1. How do you square Ishmael's concern for the murdering of oxen, birds, etc. with the butchery of the whale so recently retold?

2. How are the cannibalism of beasts and men and the carnivorousness of men parallel for Ishmael?

3. Blake's *Song of Innocence* includes a poem on the gentle

lamb; his *Songs of Experience* includes the famous "Tiger, Tiger burning bright . . ." which also asks the question "Did he who make the lamb make thee?" The answer is obvious. Do you see a parallel in *Moby-Dick?*

Dunfermline

LXVI. *The shark massacre*

1. The viciousness of nature continues to be symbolized in the sharks. How are we meant to take Queequeg's remark that "de god wat made shark must be one dam Ingin"? Why the latter term, do you think?

LXVII. *Cutting in*

1. Research question: how well did people at the time of publication know whaling, particularly the technicalities covered by this series of chapters?

LXVIII. *The blanket*

1. Ishmael also uses the term *counterpane* for the whale's skin. How is this an actual and transcendental parallel to the earlier counterpane of Queequeg and Ishmael?

2. Ishmael himself urges upon us all to be like the whale, "warm among ice" and to "live in this world without being of it." In actuality, Ishmael has been under Ahab's spell, yet has not lastingly succumbed. His objective view now must already have had some part in his experiencing then. Do you think his whale-likeness is what made Ishmael the narrator?

isinglass, integument, engraving, hieroglyphical, Agassiz, poncho

LXIX. *The funeral*

1. How does the stripped whale represent a recurrent image of terror?

2. A stronger terror lies for Ishmael in the "horrible vultureism of earth!" Explain.

3. How is the dead carcass of the whale a lesson in tradition and orthodoxy for Ishmael? Does he differentiate at all between the desirable and undesirable kind?

4. How orthodox a Presbyterian has Ishmael shown himself? Does he seem to belong at all in the Paine-Franklin-Cooper-Emerson-Thoreau-Whitman stream of American nondenominationalism?

desecrated, orthodoxy

LXX. *The sphynx*

1. Ishmael has been exclaiming at the cannibalism and vultureism of the earth for several chapters. Here Ahab soliloquizes on the same general theme. What is the difference in conclusion?

2. Ahab's thesis seems to be that the more you experience of the universe the less________you are likely to have.

3. How does Ahab's final sentence equate with Ahab's transcendentalism? Of what importance is this?

sphynx, decapitated, Holofernes and Judith, insatiate man

LXXI. *The Jereboam's story*

Ahab's soliloquy and this third of the gam series continue the story of the quest during the current concentration on extending the book to include the whale and its entire sea environs and whaling as perilous undertaking, as high art, as vital industry, and as farflung frontier. Could narrator Ishmael be trying to crowd the world, yes the universe, into one universal book? Is it likely, even possible, that he can?

1. Does Ishmael's recapitulation of the story of Gabriel suggest he believed the prophecies?

2. Are we to take seriously Gabriel's prophecy to Ahab, "thou art soon going that way"?

3. How does the ship's name allude to our story?
4. We have already had a whole series of supposed omens. List them, as completely as you can. Do you think that cumulatively they are meant to affect us, even though the single occurrences leave us unconvinced?

incorruptible, peremptorily, scaramouch, Neskyeuna Shakers, cringed, fawned, gibbering

LXXII. *The monkey-rope*

1. How had Ishmael's free will "received a mortal wound" via the monkey rope?
2. How is the monkey-rope relationship typical of most others?
3. Characteristically, whose dangers occur to Ishmael first and whose second?
4. Why is it important that Ishmael terms Queequeg "my particular friend" and "my dear comrade and twin-brother"?
5. Why should so much fuss be made over Aunt Charity's ginger?

Siamese ligature, interregnum

LXXIII. *Stubb and Flash kill a right whale; and then have a talk over him*

1. Why were the Pequod men, spermwhalers disdainful of right whales, ordered to catch a Right Whale? From whom comes the reason? Who gave the order?
2. Why should it be Stubb rather than Flask who thinks of Fedallah as the devil and who feels there's a swap of soul for Moby-Dick set between Fedallah and Ahab?
3. What is the sense of Stubb saying he'd keep ducking the devil? Is Stubb really not afraid of him?
4. Fedallah is here called a Parsee. What is a Parsee and

what are his basic beliefs? Does your answer help explain why Fedallah read palms and whale foreheads comparatively? and why Fedallah seemed the lengthened shadow of Ahab?

orlop, Beelzebub, Locke, Kant, panniers, Laplandish

LXXIV. *The sperm whale's head—contrasted view*

1. What does Ishmael mean by saying it is the eyes that make the front of a man?

2. What are the essential differences between sight in man and whale? Why is Ishmael so interested in the comparison, do you suppose?

3. Ishmael speaks of the "helpless perplexity of volition, in which their divided and diametrically opposite powers of vision must involve them." Does this suggest that for Ishmael whales have a will? a free will?

Herschel, portcullis

LXXV. *The right whale's head—contrasted view*

1. What do you think Ishmael means when he finds the sperm whale's head expressive of "a speculative indifference to death" and the right whale's one of "an enormous practical resolution in facing death"? What does he mean by his comparison of them to a Stoic (right) and "a Platonian, who might have taken up Spinoza in his latter years" (sperm)?

2. Is Ishmael, as a transcendentalist or idealist, seeing manifestations of spirit as pervading all things? Give reasons for your answer.

imprecate, scimetar-shaped, cursorily, Purchas, farthingale

LXXVI. *The battering-ram*

1. Ishmael is obviously building verisimilitude for the physical prowess of the sperm whale in general, Moby-Dick in

particular. How does he already hint at psychological verisimilitude as well?

2. Why does he capitalize Truth?

Lais

LXXVII. *The Great Heidelberg Tun*

1. Research Question: of what use is the sperm whale's spermaceti oil to him?

2. Cite all the reasons you can why Ishmael deliberately interrupts his story for all the details of whales and whaling, remembering that Melville added all these to the originally simpler whaling story many still prefer so much that they edit the book accordingly.

unctuous, tendinous, Tierce, pelisse

LXXVIII. *Cistern and buckets*

1. Queequeg performs another unbelievable rescue. Why do you suppose he keeps being the one?

2. What does the concluding allusion of falling into Plato's honey head signify, generally and specifically for narrator Ishmael?

3. Why do you suppose Ahab is unaccounted for at these doings?

LXXIX. *The pra[i]rie*

1. Ishmael says, "I try all things; I achieve what I can." Is this statement true of his living? of his narrating?

2. Why do you think Ishmael uses the prairie with which to compare the sperm whale's forehead?

3. The sperm whale testifies to the grandeur of God's creation. Is this what Ishmael means when he says, "you feel the

Deity and the dread powers more forcibly than in beholding any other subject in living nature"?

4. Why does Ishmael call himself "unlettered Ishmael"?

phrenological, cupola, Phidias, Melancthon, Lavater, Champollion

LXXX. *The nut*

1. Is it physiologically possible, as Ishmael holds, that the great size of the sperm whale's spinal cord compensates for the smallness of his brain?

LXXXI. *The Pequod meets the Virgin*

1. What biblical parallel is the case of the *Virgin* supposed to suggest?

2. What parallel is there between the whale chased this time and Ahab? What is the whale supposed to illustrate?

3. Why is a wounded whale limited in the depth and time he can sound?

4. What attributes of this whale made the fight so unequal that Ishmael calls it murder for lighting men's gay bridals and churches "that preach unconditional inoffensiveness by all to all"?

pod, egress, yaw, tilbury

LXXXII. *The honor and glory of whaling*

1. Why should Ishmael be at such pains to suggest that Perseus' Minotaur and St. George's Dragon, as well as assorted other beasts of antiquity, were whales?

2. Does the incarnation of Vishnoo as a whale relate to your answer above?

intrepidly, St. George, Ezekiel, Philistines, Dagon, Brahma

LXXXIII. *Jonah historically regarded*

1. What is Ishmael's position on the historicity of the Jonah story? Of what importance is it? Why does he bring it up at all, and at this point, do you suppose?

2. What does Ishmael mean by the "foolish pride of rearm"?

Arion, exegetist

LXXXIV. *Pitchpoling*

1. What qualities are required for pitchpoling? Why is Stubb particularly suited to pitchpoling?

Cleopatra, Actium, Monongahela

LXXXV. *The fountain*

1. What interior evidence for dating the composition of *Moby-Dick* is contained in this chapter? How would one check it? Can you think of other things in the book which would date it in a general way?

2. Earlier we spoke of necessity, free will and chance in the hunting of whales. What factor is added here to necessity?

3. Ishmael comments on the voicelessness of the whale by reminding us that "Seldom have I known any profound being that had anything to say to this world, unless forced to stammer out something by way of getting a living." Does this apply to author Melville?

4. What has modern research found regarding the make-up of the whale's spout?

5. How does the conclusion of the chapter characterize Ishmael philosophically? religiously? Does your answer support his choice as narrator?

contingent, anomalous, vermicelli, spiracle, Pyrrho, Dante

LXXXVI. *The tail*

1. How can Ishmael attribute contemptuousness to the sperm whale's use of his tail in fighting man?

2. How does the whale compare with the elephant in size, tail, etc.?

confluent, Titanism, Eckerman, Goethe, Angelo, prehensile, Darmonodes, peaking

LXXXVII. *The grand armada*

1. Trace on the map Ahab's intended voyage before meeting Moby-Dick.

2. What two unusual events occurred in the Straits of Sunda?

3. Ishmael holds "there is no folly of the beast of the earth which is not infinitely outdone by the madness of men." What factors are at work in the comparison?

4. How does Ishmael compare his own center of being to that center of the whale armada into which they have been pulled by a whale? Compare Ishmael in this to Queequeg, Stubb, Starbuck and Ahab.

5. Again Starbuck's boat has the narrowest of escapes. Almost it would seem that not merely the narrator has to survive, but that all must. Does Ishmael comment on this? Why or why not?

Malacca, Birmah, Sumatra, Bally (Bali), Java, Sunda, proas, corsairs, Kentledge, stun-sail, reticule, vicissitudes

LXXXVIII. *Schools and schoolmasters*

1. What two kinds of sperm whale schools are there?
2. Why are all old whales lone ones, according to Ishmael?
3. What difference in defense are there in the two schools?

4. Why does Ishmael constantly speak of the schools here, and whales generally, in human terms?

embonpoint, Bashaw, Vidocq, Lothario

LXXXIX. *Fast-fish and loose-fish*

1. What is the simple whaling code regarding possession?
2. Does the case Ishmael cites base itself on that code?
3. How does Ishmael prove that this simple code is really at the core of all jurisprudence? Give parallels of your own.
4. What is the significance that the broker's name is Mordecai?
5. What is the allusion to Mexico as an eventual Loose-Fish to the United States?
6. Why does Ishmael call individual rights, liberties and beliefs Loose-fish?

Justinian's Pandects, doxology

XC. *Heads or tails*

1. Surely Ishmael's sense of humor comes to the fore here. Cite other instances of that humor, especially in the present section on whales and whaling.

Cinque Ports, emoluments, sinecure, fobbing, Plowdon

XCI. *The Pequod meets the Rose-Bud*

This is the fifth of the series of gams that carry the story line through this "technical" section. The first three were Nantucketers, the fourth German, and this one French. As such they represent the dominance of the industry by American, particularly Nantucket, whalers. They also serve as extension from the Pequod's cosmopolitan crew to the international nature of whaling and whalers.

1. Do you think the French captain, an ex-Cologne manu-

facturer, did not know why he was going after blasted and sick whales?

2. How was the code regarding fish involved here?

attar-of-rose, Crappoes, anathernas, ostentatiously, diddled

XCII. *Ambergris*

1. Why does Ishmael use the simile "similar to that [savor] arising from excavating an old city graveyard, for the foundations of a Lying-in Hospital"? and why the analogy of in the middle ages supposedly detecting a Jew "by the nose"?

2. How does knowing things by their contraries apply here?

pastiles, Mecca, St. Peter's claret, dyspepsia, Brandreth's pills, Paracelsus

XCIII. *The castaway*

This episode about little Pip overboard is one of the few aside from gams to thread the story through this section, preparing also for subsequent events.

1. How would you characterize Ishmael's attitude toward Negroes? Remember to add to this chapter his delineation of Daggoo, his remarks regarding slave ships, etc.

2. How do Tashtego and Stubb show up in Pip's jumping overboard, remembering Tashtego's own rescue from the sinking whalehead?

3. What is most intolerable about being overboard, without other complications, that affected Pip on his second jump?

4. Ishmael says that in his madness Pip saw God in all his primal Wisdom. How is this madness related to what Ahab sees in himself and others also see in him?

5. Ishmael holds that heaven's sense is above man's reason. Of what is this evidence in him?

6. Ishmael reveals that he too will encounter an abandonment like Pip. Of course he is narrating sanely, so evidently

he will not go mad. Why does he reveal this future occurrence here, do you suppose?

poltroon, execrations, inexorable

Let us use this chapter as illustration of how the question guide looks both backward and forward, as it considers present events.

1. The answer would surely be favorable. In addition to the suggested evidence, think of Stubb and Fleece (Chapter LXIII), earlier treatment of Pip, the crew generally. Add others yourself.

2. Both are merciful, though they are in the passion of the chase and naturally hate to part with its object: the whale as such and the income he represents.

3. Ishmael says of being afloat that "the awful loneliness is intolerable," etc. (4th paragraph from the end). Think of this statement also in terms of the pithy concluding paragraph.

4. Pip sees God beyond reason, in a way "sane" people do not because their logic helps them not to have to see God in all his terrible beauty, something they might well not be able to survive. Ahab's madness, conversely, is in great part self-inflicted even though the hand of fate seems, and is, strongly in it. We could say it is not Ahab's madness which drives him, but that in him which is yet self-aware and which he must constantly subvert. Pip is all affection and obedience, Ahab all anger and defiance. Finally, in Pip's madness Ahab sees only the senselessness of the universal injustice, and so Pip, in more ways than one, becomes Ahab's son. (Compare Emily Dickinson's poem "Much madness is divinest sense")

5. Ishmael's opinion shows his belief in the essential reason and rightness of the universe, its terrors notwithstanding. He manifests balance regarding the serious and the comic, good and evil, Ahab and Moby-Dick, fate and free will, detachment and involvement.

6. Ishmael's revelation augments, even as it seems to lessen,

suspense. It also places Pip's experience as comparable to Ishmael's coming one.

XCIV. *A squeeze of the hand*

1. What "horrible oath" did Ishmael forget when kneading the sperm?

2. What has Ishmael learned about "attainable felicity" and the intellect and the fancy?

3. Is Ishmael's squeezing of his fellow kneader's hands a result of men in only one another's company for months and years on end, of seeing the whales in domestic bliss, of a kind of semi-mystic experience, or some combination of these and/or others?

4. There is danger even in unexpected places in whaling. What are those of the try-room?

Constantine's bath, mollifier, acerbities, slobgollion, gurry, glutinous, nippers, squilgee

XCV. *The cassock*

1. Where does the cone that furnishes the mincer's cassock come from? How do you know? Of what significance is this?

cassock, mincer, investiture

XCVI. *The try-works*

1. What is the try-works?

2. How does Ishmael use the title also as a pun?

3. His telling of his momentary hallucination in half-doze almost falls into dialogue with himself. Ishmael has not figured in ship's dialogue since Chapter XXI, Going Aboard. Why do you think this is so?

4. Ishmael's moment of fire-brought terror is brought to an end by the thought that the true fire, the sun, will return at morning. Still he will not gloss over the dark side of life.

On whom and what does he call for help against this side of life? How does his compare with Ahab's facing of the same dark side?

cycloid, plethoric, Hydriote, Canaris, Cowper, Young, Pascal, Rousseau, Rabelais

XCVII. *The lamp*

1. How does the whaleman live in his own light?

XCVIII. *Stowing down and clearing up*

The beginning of the chapter reviews the stages of whaling already treated and turns then to the final stage—decanting the oil into casks and stowing them in the hold.

1. How and why does the glory of whaling become a "weary thing"?
2. Why should the crew be so different upon cleaning ship after a catch has been disposed?
3. What does the allusion to Pythagoras mean?

XCIX. *The doubloon*

1. How were Ishmael's thoughts at the wheel a preparation for Ahab and the mates soliloquizing on the doubloon?
2. What is for Ahab the center of the doubloon? Why?
3. What does the doubloon signify to Starbuck?
4. What is the essential character of Stubb's interpretation of the zodiac as the round of human life? Why is he picked to string commentary among the remaining viewers of the gold piece?
5. What does the doubloon mean to Flask? to the Manxman? to Queequeg? to Fedallah?
6. How is Pip's comment really central to all the wisest of the lot? How does its conclusion, unheard by even Stubb, seem to be also prophecy?

C. *Leg and arm*

In this 6th of the gams the *Pequod* speaks an English ship, continuing the microcosm-of-mankind connotation. The application to Ahab's quest once more becomes central.

1. What does the levity of Captain Boomer after the loss of his arm show?

2. Why did Boomer not lower for Moby-Dick again?

3. How does Dr. Bunger explain men's notion of malice in whales? What medical fact does he cite as evidence?

4. What happens when Bunger tries his humor on Ahab? Is Ishmael who records the scene aware of all the implications? How could he know what went on, since only Ahab and his crew visited the *Enderby*?

hydrophobia

CI. *The decanter*

1. What does Ishmael's later gam add to our conception of him as a person?

2. Is the style here in keeping with the subject? What can you say of this generally in the book?

3. What does Ishmael mean when he says he studied the Dutch whaler supply list for "transcendental and Platonic application"? Why should he use both adjectives?

anti-scorbutic

CII. *A bower in the Arsacides*

1. Why does Ishmael, addressing himself by name twice, warn himself against thinking he is a Jonah?

2. How does the weaver analogy here parallel the chapter on the mat-maker?

Arsacides, vertu, Damocles

CIII. *Measurement of the whaler's skeleton*

1. Why should the skeleton of the whale remind him of the keel and rib structure of a boat?

2. Ishmael says once more that no one can do justice to the whale who has not seen him (experienced directly, not vicariously) in his context (own environs). Compare the latter notion to that in Emerson's poem "Each and All."

3. Why does Ishmael call the priest's children who stole the whale's small vertebrae for playing marbles "cannibal urchins"?

Pompey's Pillar

CIV. *The fossil whale*

As so often, Ishmael hymns the grandeur of the whale and his sweeps through the vastnesses of deeps and ages. In Whitman's words, "I am afoot with my vision!" These chapters form his peroration, in which he rhapsodizes every aspect of whales and whaling, as his theme expands "throughout the whole universe, not excluding its suburbs," with pre-historic and post-historic time included.

1. Why do you think Ishmael feels that the full dictionary must be brought into play for "the leviathan"?

2. "To produce a mighty book, you must choose a mighty theme." What does he have in mind, specifically and generally?

3. What does Ishmael mean, "time began with man"?

4. "I am horror-struck at this antemosaic, unsourced existence of the unspeakable terrors of the whale, which, having been before all time, must needs exist after all humane ages are over." How does this horror relate to Ahab's "monomaniac purpose"?

5. In order for Ishmael to understand and judge Ahab (as he continuously does, in the best sense of the word) he must

really face the same universe and as nakedly as Ahab. Does he? How or how not?

antediluvian, chirography, condor's quill, antichronical, pre-adamite, antemosaic, Denderah, planisphere

CV. *Does the whale's magnitude diminish?—will he perish?*

1. Here Ishmael disbelieves naturalists on the great size of whales. Yet earlier he believes that the minotaur, etc. were whales. How do these two notions equate?

2. Ishmael feels the whale will not be exterminated like the buffalo because whaling is so different. What about the possibility in terms of today's mechanized whaling?

Aldrovandus, Lacepede, cachalot

CVI. *Ahab's leg*

The decks are cleared of whales, actual and literary. From now to the end Ahab's quest and latterly the chase itself consume all our attention.

1. Why did Ishmael not mention Ahab's wrenching of his ivory leg shortly before sailing? Would this have helped us to understand how the monomania grew in him or not?

2. Ahab thought, "both the ancestry and posterity of Grief go further than the ancestry and posterity of Joy." How does this sentiment compare with those of Ishmael toward the close of Chapter LXXXVII (short paragraph beginning "And thus, though surrounded by circle upon circle . . .") and his feelings about felicity while squeezing sperm (Chapter XCIV)?

thwart, bruited, synod

CVII. *The carpenter*

1. Does humbleness of origin or place deny originality to man, according to Ishmael? Does this add something to the recurrent natural democracy theme?

2. How does the carpenter view all things? How does your answer square with the soliloquies on the doubloon?

3. How was the carpenter "a stript abstract; an unfractional integral"? Cite similar kinds of persons from your own experience, actual or vicarious.

athwartships, belaying pin, vermilion, all-ramifying, *multum in parvo*

CVIII. *Ahab and the carpenter*

1. Why does Ahab call the carpenter "manmaker"?

2. Why does Ahab wish to order the kind of mechanical man he itemizes?

3. Why does Ahab call the lantern thrust at him by the carpenter a thief-catcher?

4. What does Ahab mean that just as he can still feel his amputated leg, so a whole person can stand in one's stead? Is he referring to an alter ego? Is this a sign of his schizophrenic tendency? Is he thinking of (or is Ishmael implying) Fedallah?

5. Ahab chafes under the necessary dependence on others. Compare this with Ishmael's thoughts about the monkey rope (Chapter LXXII) and while squeezing sperm (Chapter XCIV). Why should we be constantly making comparisons between the two?

ferrule, hop-poles, Prometheus, spavined

CIX. *Ahab and Starbuck in the cabin*

1. What does Ahab mean that he himself is aleak?

2. How is Starbuck's reference to the owners as meaningful for himself as for Ahab?

3. How is Starbuck's advice, "let Ahab beware of Ahab," also as significant for himself as for Ahab?

4. Why do *you* think Ahab changed his mind and ordered the Burtons lowered and the hold broken out?

Burtons, Bashee Isles, Niphon, Matsmai, Sikoke, close-reef

CX. *Queequeg in his coffin*

1. What is the import of Ishmael's calling Queequeg's near-death an approach "to his endless end"?

2. What is "the immortal health in him"?

3. Why do you suppose Pip and his raving about his own cowardice is brought in just at this point, when Queequeg is trying out his coffin?

4. What was Queequeg's "conceit"? Why is it termed so?

5. Queequeg in effect says will is all. How is Stubb his opposite?

tierce, shooks, demijohn

CXI. *The Pacific*

The entrance of the *Pequod* into the Pacific prompts in narrator Ishmael a rhapsody much like the earlier one at the Masthead. The individual spirit seems to merge with the universal all, yet remain inviolately aware of both identity and identification. For Ahab it means the testing of his intent alternately by beauty and balm and by typhoon terror. The one saps, the other supercharges. Therefore it is in the middle ground of the line that the epic drama plays itself out, with combatants at full advantage and nature's influence in neutralized restraint.

1. As Bryant in "Thanatopsis" sees the earth as one great grave, Ishmael here images the deep as one; Ishmael, however, uses dreams as metaphor while Bryant uses them as simile. What difference in outlook is represented?

2. Why does Ishmael invoke the god Pan?
3. Why would Ahab cry out "Stern all!"?

Ephesian, Potters' Fields

CXII. *The blacksmith*

1. Such stories as Perth's life history are not unusual. Is his made part of the book because it drove him to whaling? Does he parallel Ahab?
2. Does Ishmael in speaking of Death, mean the universe is unjust? How do you know?
3. What are "interior compunctions to suicide"?

CXIII. *The forge*

1. Do you think Ahab's comment regarding madness to Perth has anything to do with Perth's life history?
2. Why does Ahab insist upon forging the twelve rods together into his own harpoon?
3. When Perth asks whether the spear is for the white whale, why does Ahab answer "For the white fiend!"?
4. What is the importance of Ahab's saying, ". . . I now neither shave, sup, nor pray till . . ."?
5. Whom does Ahab invoke in baptizing his harpoon? What does this say of his attitude toward God?
6. Why is Pip's laugh termed a mockery?

pike-head

CXIV. *The gilder*

1. This is the latest in a series of moments unifying fact and fancy, reason and faith; merging contraries in the no-man's land between waking and sleeping, of dreams here though of nightmares elsewhere. Can you recall others in the series? What is their function?
2. Who or what is "the gilder" of the title?

3. With no one on stage, Ishmael depicts four ages of man. How does his outlook compare with the famous one of Jaques in "As You Like It"?

4. Why should it be just Starbuck and Stubb whose thoughts Ishmael here has reflected in the ocean's mirror?

CXV. *The Pequod meets the Bachelor*

Gam No. 7 continues the testing of Ahab, arousing his resolve anew despite the longing for things which content other men. Each test is also another age old warning and opportunity to turn back, to repent like Jonah. Or does God harden the heart of Ahab as he hardened the heart of Pharaoh?

1. Why should it be such a full ship that is also such a merry one? Why named the *Bachelor?*

2. What irony lurks in Ahab's comment, "How wondrous familiar is a fool!"?

3. What is the significance of Ahab taking the vial from his pocket?

CXVI. *The dying whale*

1. What does Ahab mean by "here, too, life dies sunwards full of faith"?

2. How does Ahab's address to "thou dark Hindoo half of nature, who of drowned bones hast builded thy separate throne somewhere in the heart of these unverdured seas" relate to Fedallah and his (Parsee) religion? Does this suggest that Ahab has deliberately forsaken Christianity? Why should the fire be feminine and a queen (any Christian parallel)?

3. How does Ahab's schizophrenic bent manifest itself here in the moral as well as the mental sphere?

orisons

CXVII. *The whale watch*

1. What is the prophecy of Fedallah for Ahab? for himself?

2. Why should Ahab be dreaming of the prophecy? Why does Fedallah know at once what he had dreamt again?

3. Why should Ahab seem to believe Fedallah's prophecy?

Asphaltites

CXVIII. *The quadrant*

Each test and turnabout chance for Ahab represents the like for his crew. Although Starbuck is foremost in command and responsibility, none are exempt, including Ishmael whose self-effacement for narrative reasons must not blind us to his own share in the collective blame.

1. What is Ahab looking into, symbolically, when he stares straight into the sun's eye?

2. Why does Ahab dash the quadrant to the deck and abjure its use?

3. Explain the reaction (look) of Fedallah. Why "fatalistic despair that seemed meant for himself"?

4. What is suggested here as the power Fedallah has and does not have? Of what importance do you hold the limitation?

5. Once more the reactions of only Starbuck and Stubb are given. Why should these two and their viewpoints be stressed so? What are their viewpoints?

quadrant, effulgences, burning-glass, Horatii

CXIX. *The candles*

1. The opening paragraph presents a series of sweeping generalizations, a favorite rhetorical pattern of the narrator. Note the one which makes up most of the fourth paragraph in Chapter CXV. Can you remember other such? What char-

acteristics are common to them in noun and adjective patterns, in connectives, in punctuation, in rhythms, and length of elements, in repetition vs. variation, etc.?

2. Why does narrator Ishmael here invoke "Mene, Mene, Tekel Upharsin" from the Book of Daniel (5:25-28, the original handwriting on the wall)?

3. What does Starbuck find odd about Ahab's boat being stove in?

4. How do Stubb's song, his oath and his interpretation of the corpusants all contribute to your understanding of him?

5. What new recognition regarding his quest does Ahab reach during his apostrophe to fire?

6. What does Ahab mean by "In the midst of the personified impersonal, a personality stands here"?

7. Does Ahab worship the fire as such?

8. What is Fedallah's function here?

9. How is a one-legged older man able to conquer a mate and crew at least momentarily convinced that God is against Ahab?

10. What is their "terror of dismay"?

doxology, supernal

CXX. *The deck towards the end of the first night watch*

1. Is there an advance in Ahab's control of Starbuck here? Why or why not?

2. Why does Ahab translate all exterior happenings into internal terms?

3. Why is Ahab at the helm here?

CXXI. *Midnight—the forecastle bulwarks*

1. Test Stubb's reasoning that they were actually in no danger during the lightning tapers, and then decide whether this jibes with his comments in Chapter CXIX.

lucifers, Aquarius

CXXII. *Midnight aloft—thunder and lightning*

1. What is added and/or confirmed here in the character of Tashtego?

2. This series of chapters (CXIV-CXXII) begins with bright Pacific day, and goes through sundown to midnight, thus paralleling an earlier series (XXXV-XL). Is there any parallel deeper than this surface one?

CXXIII. *The musket*

1. Does Starbuck's reasoning build up a convincing case against Ahab?

2. Is Starbuck conscious of any alternative to killing Ahab?

3. What does Ishmael mean us to think of right and wrong here—that Starbuck should have shot him? How do you know?

4. In retrospect, where was Starbuck's real failure of nerve? Why?

spasmodic, vicissitudes

CXXIV. *The needle*

1. The turning of the compass needles was not accidental. If the reader is to take this and similar happenings as signs or omens, what can we say of Ishmael's view of the nature of omens?

2. Why is there a paragraph devoted to the reactions of the entire crew to the reversed needles?

3. Why is Ahab's pride described as "fatal"? Do all of Ishmael's verbal signs like this point to the doom of the voyage?

kelson, level loadstone, prudential

CXXV. *The log and line*

1. Of what is it a sign that Ahab refuses to take the Manxman's warning regarding the deterioration of the log line?

2. Ahab tells the heavens that they have abandoned Pip? What is the reader to think? How do you know?

3. How would you characterize Ahab's punning on man/Man?

4. In taking Pip by the hand and into his cabin to live, Ahab calls the gods "oblivious of suffering" and man the opposite: what is he in effect saying of himself?

5. How are the madnesses of Ahab and Pip different, beyond the Manxman's calling one strength, the other weakness?

6. Is there here an implication that one can be too strong, too brave, as well as too cowardly?

oblique, festoon

CXXVI. *The life-buoy*

1. The loss of the sailor from the crow's nest and the sinking of the dried out life-buoy could happen anytime. What is the significance of their occurrence here?

2. Why should it be Queequeg who suggests making a life-buoy cask out of his coffin?

Herod's murdered Innocents, presaged, innuendos, batten, Aroostook, cruppered

CXXVII. *The deck*

1. Why does Ahab say "The gods again" to the carpenter's retort "But I do not mean anything, sir. I do as I do"?

2. What "gravedigger in the play sings, spade in hand"? Why should Ahab be made to recall this famous scene for himself and us?

3. Why does Ahab become impatient and ask the carpenter to "get these traps out of sight"?

4. Is Ahab approaching a Platonic notion of reality in his soliloquy here?

5. What is the significance of Ahab asking (is he uncon-

sciously punning now?), "Can it be that in some spiritual sense the coffin is, after all, but an immortality-preserver"?

oakum, ferrule, Titans

CXXVIII. *The Pequod meets the Rachel*

1. What is significant about Stubb's change in attitude regarding the Rachel's captain's request?
2. Why should it be the Manxman who alludes to the previous night's seal-cries as being really the cries of the lost seamen's spirits?
3. Why was this ship named the Rachel, called "the child-seeking Rachel" in the next chapter (Genesis 30, 35)?

unenervated

CXXIX. *The cabin*

1. Why should Pip be like a cure to Ahab's malady, and why should Ahab hold that malady to be "his most desired health"?
2. Is Ahab being blasphemous when he says to Pip "So: God for ever bless thee; and if it come to that,—God for ever save thee, let what will befall"? What does your answer suggest regarding Ahab's religious belief?
3. Why is Pip again and again made to rail against cowards, aside from enlisting personal sympathy?

CXXX. *The hat*

1. Why did Ahab no more return to his cabin?
2. Why should Fedallah be ceaselessly shuddering, when Ahab is not at all?
3. What does Platonist Ishmael probably mean by describing Ahab and Fedallah as substance and shadow?
4. Why do you think Ahab has Starbuck pull him aloft and secure the line?

5. What is the significance of the hat snatching? How many such occurrences have now been noted?

Tarquin, Tanaquil

CXXXI. *The Pequod meets the Delight*

1. Why does Ahab command "Up helm!" just when he does?

2. The peroration of Father Mapple's sermon is an apostrophe to delight. Does it apply here?

CXXXII. *The symphony*

1. Ishmael's metaphors are hardly ever, if ever, mere comparisons. Why does he use the Samson metaphor here (Judges 16)? How do the feminine air and masculine sea develop the metaphor?

2. A tear was vital to the Ancient Mariner. What difference between his and Ahab's here?

3. What is Ahab's long speech to Starbuck about his past meant to do for us?

4. Why do you suppose Ahab married a young girl at 50 only to leave ("widow") her next day?

5. Once again Ahab mentions God, several times; is it in blasphemy? Of what importance is this?

6. Would this be the time to try dissuading Ahab from his quest? Why or why not?

7. What does Ahab mean when he asks "Is Ahab, Ahab?"

8. Why does Starbuck steal away in "despair"?

9. Why is ever-present Fedallah not there when Starbuck is, but replaces Starbuck?

10. As Ahab and Starbuck defy and default on each chance for reversal what happens to the likelihood of such reversal? Do you think this may be Ishmael's way of accounting naturally for the hardening of their hearts?

11. Why the title of this chapter? Is it related to the previous one, the last gam, with the *Delight?*

Samson, cantankerous, Albicore

CXXXIII. *The chase—first day*

1. Is it important that Ahab himself sights Moby-Dick? Then his charts have been right; how does that differ from Jonah and his whale?
2. Ahab tells Starbuck to stay aboard; why?
3. What was the effect of lowering after Moby-Dick on Fedallah? Why, do you think?
4. Why did Fedallah take Moby-Dick's jaw-assault so well?
5. Is there any reason for the allusion to Antiochus's elephants (Maccabees, 6:34), noting also the elephant reference in the paragraph beginning "Dragged into Stubb's boat . . ."?
6. What does Ahab mean that Starbuck is Stubb reversed and the two are all mankind? Does this remark relate to the frequent appearance of the two successively, often at ends of chapters? Why or why not?
7. When Ahab is told that his stove boat is an omen he says "if the gods think to speak outright to man," they will do so, "not shake their heads and give an old wives' darkling hint." Can their speaking be outright by reason of cumulative, rather than immediate, outrightness?
8. Why does Ahab promise them all money if he himself raises Moby-Dick on the day of his killing?

palpable, dog-vane, nautilus shells, argosy, pennons, Jupiter, Europa, Eddystone

CXXXIV. *The chase—second day*

1. What does narrator Ishmael mean when he says "The Land of Fate had snatched all their souls"?

2. Why do you suppose Moby-Dick acted in a sense so unpredictably, turning again and again upon the boats?

3. This time in his attempt to dissuade Ahab Starbuck does it "In Jesus' name"; Why, do you think? Is Starbuck right in finding "all good angels mobbing thee with warnings"? Compare with Macbeth, Chillingworth in *The Scarlet Letter* and Montresor in "The Cask of Amontillado."

4. In his reply Ahab alludes to his late affinity for Starbuck; has that affinity been returned?

5. Does the loss of Fedallah say anything about the so-called "omens"?

pertinacious, heliotrope glance

CXXXV. *The chase—third day*

1. Ahab says he only feels, that thinking is God's privilege; is this true? Of what importance is this comment to our understanding of Ahab?

2. How mad is Ahab at this point?

3. Ahab says, "all the things that most exasperate and outrage mortal man, all these things are bodiless, but only bodiless as objects [that is, in themselves], not as agents [that is they have the identity of instruments]" How does this apply to Moby-Dick?

4. Why does Ishmael say that at the third raising of Moby-Dick "three shrieks went up as if the tongues of fire had voiced it"?

5. Ahab's sense of fatality in parting a third time from Starbuck must come as a result of something; what, do you suppose?

6. Did Starbuck expect Ahab to heed his tears? Does Starbuck's rhetoric betray him here? What can you tell from it?

7. Whose voice warned Ahab of the sharks?

8. Who in Ahab's boat makes the remark about the sharks? Does this sound like one of his phantom crew?

9. How mad is Ahab at the end? Is he to be held responsible for his actions?

10. Does Ahab feel himself to be, and act like, a free agent at the end?

11. Does Ahab raise to tragic heights at his end? Why or why not?

12. Is Fedallah's prophecy entirely fulfilled? Elijah's?

13. What is the hawk hammered to the masthead by Tashtego intended to symbolize?

14. Why is it "five thousand years ago"?

Monadnock, Fata Morgana

Epilogue

1. Why is the epigraph of the epilogue taken from Job (Chapters 40 and 41)?

2. Why should it have been Fedallah's replacement that is saved? Why do you suppose Ahab chose Ishmael as the replacement? What does Ishmael's lone comment (last chapter) show of his relationship to Ahab? Of his feelings?

3. Why should it be Queequeg's coffin turned into life buoy that saves Ishmael?

4. Is there any significance to the fact that the actual chase took three days, with Ishmael sucked in by death but saved?

5. The nature of the rescue is plainly miraculous, leading to the question with which Ishmael and we began, "Why me?" What would you now answer, first in terms of him surviving, second in terms of *all* the others perishing? Is the parallel of the Ancient Mariner and his crew applicable? Why do the owners share in the disaster?

6. The hand of fate being so strong here, does it point to the possibility that as Ishmael was destined to survive, Ahab was destined to try God? If so, what about man's freedom of the will? Is everything then predestined and the whole book an essay in determinism?

7. Ahab fails his basic Christian command; does Ishmael manifest his adherence to it?

8. Would your understanding of the book be the same if the epilogue were omitted, as it was in the first English edition?

Sketches of Principal Characters

★ ISHMAEL

"Call me Ishmael" at once announces the narrator of *Moby-Dick*. The reader accepts the author's chosen point of view, here third person Ishmael, and expects to witness the events through the eyes, the experience of the narrator, including the conscious and subconscious past experiences, the attitudes and the mood of the moment, he brings to any given situation. We soon realize that Ishmael is an older and wiser person narrating and interpreting events experienced as a young man. We often get both his reactions at the time and his subsequent reflective understanding of them. The crowning reason for this dual point of view does not present itself until the very end.

Ishmael seems destined for survival; therefore he must have something of whatever potential for survival before embarking on the *Pequod*. The early shore chapters represent Ishmael's look at that potential. The voyage chapters explore his relationship to Ahab and Ahab's monomaniac quest to ascertain why he of all the crew should survive. Many are of greater physical prowess, some more courageous, a few at least of equal moral fiber. Ishmael appraises all his capabilities—physical, emotional, intellectual, ethical, religious—and with rare modesty, structurally and stylistically attained through the focus on Ahab and crew, arrives at his answer. Ishmael's qualities for survival emerge cumulatively, as the question guide points up: his Calvinistic Presbyterian background; his education and teaching; his reading; his sea experiences; his sense of humor; his aesthetic detachment; his "Platonist" outlook—to name some outstanding influences. What emerges only impliedly is Ishmael the storyteller, narrator, and interpreter*—in short, the artist capable of recreating the events themselves and their fullest context, both in all their universality. Ishmael becomes an Ancient Mariner who must tell his story, partly to fulfill its destined telling, partly to expiate his own involvement in Ahab's demonic and demoralizing experience without easy didactic judgment, with understanding of a dare few could rise to, and yet with the demonstrable conviction that Ahab's view is intellectually erroneous and spiritually evil. Ishmael, the Ancient Mariner, is also Melville, who must try the story in such cosmic inclusiveness that it is bound to fail, attempting as it does the impossible. Compensation lies in having dared with Ahab even to damnation, and dared himself to compress a transcendental universe within the covers of a single book.

★ STARBUCK

Was ever a character introduced so damningly and yet so gloriously as Starbuck. From the first the stamp of failure is placed irrevocably upon him. Suspense lies only in how and with what awareness he will fail. The glory lies of course in that as a man he has within him that divine absolute which alone makes all men equal and which periodically proves

* The point of view is strikingly caught in the skull-shaped Steuben glass design, the quest experienced through Ishmael's mind.

how individuals with utter freedom would in its misuse lessen the freedom of others, witness Ahab.

Why does Starbuck rate the distinction of such an introduction? Because he is courageous despite his fears. He dares the worst the sea can offer though he has strongest ties to home, wife and children. He has a good mind, one that forever gives him pause, pause long enough for failure of the moral fiber as reason falters into rationalization.

The first such pause and failure come on the quarterdeck, when Ahab pledges all hands to hunt the white whale to his death. Starbuck protests, subsides, submits. As Ahab through the months strengthens himself in his resolve, Starbuck weakens in his opposition, from protest to persuasion to mere pleading. When the corpusants have all the crew in terror of Ahab, Starbuck fails to take advantage of the opening. Even the seemingly climactic scene when Starbuck takes down the musket is foredoomed to failure: Starbuck is right in thinking one murder does not justify another, much less one merely preventive; but his failure of nerve extends as well to not placing Ahab in chains, which is not only his shipboard right, but also his legal and moral responsibility. He knows Ahab would not have hesitated to fire the same musket at him, had it become necessary. "I misdoubt me that I disobey my God in obeying him!"

Yet Starbuck is close to Ahab. He is all kinship for an Ahab torn between the call of the whale and the pull of home. Like Ahab too, he is meditative, although not given to universals. He has the mind which understands its own dilemma, bleeds in despair at his own impotence of will, and, conversely, tastes the irony in Ahab's strength of will toward an evil intent, yet cannot help admire his courage.

★ STUBB

Seldom among men are physical and mental prowess equal. Ahab says of Starbuck and Stubb "Ye two are the opposite poles of one thing; Starbuck is Stubb reversed, and Stubb is Starbuck; and ye two are all mankind." And the two in their separate irresolves come latterly more often together to share comment upon Ahab and his quest.

Stubb too fails from the very first, an easy victim of the kick of Ahab, which he can only frustratedly return in the abstract terms of dream at an inverted pyramid of Ahab's leg, ship's gunwale and the deck. Thereafter he is Ahab's, but that is no great matter as he invokes his handy fatalism, comes also to admire Ahab's courage, usually mistaking it for mere devil-may-care. He and Starbuck are alike in impotence of  will: with Stubb it is too little thought, shrugging off questions and doubts with it's all fate, so let's be jolly; with Starbuck it is too much thought, of the squirrel cage kind, frittering the same doubts and questions into rationalized inaction. The two are alike, yet complementary, as Ahab holds.

Stubb shrugs, but readily admits to fear. His prowess, like Starbuck's, stems from knowledge of that fear. His heedlessness is tempered by a humanity seldom allowed out. One time of its appearance is his command to cut the line and so save little Pip; another, his insistence that they must help the *Rachel*'s Captain find his lost son, though he quite gives in to Ahab's orders saying otherwise. Stubb is a second mate in fact and spirit.

★ QUEEQUEG

Queequeg seems to emerge as example of natural man and innate goodness. The view of him as such is probably overly romantic. In a sense, Daggoo and Tashtego also manifest the quality. Queequeg shows beyond the make-up of these two, the background and breeding of his royal stock. And this shows up white pretenders to civilization and colored savage imitators alike.

His is a physical prowess second to none aboard the *Pe-*

quod. He is not only the most skilled harpooner, he is also the best swimmer, the coolest under fire (and under water!). His devotion to his God, especially during the "Ramadan" peculiar to his faith, and its evident extension to the love of his fellowman (witness risking his life for the young "bumpkin" who had just mimicked him) puts the products of the Christian tradition quite to shame.

Pagan Queequeg and Christian Ishmael strike up a friendship whose roots lie deep in mutual respect and gradually in love. They are boatmates, they are sharers of the monkey-rope—both life and death dependencies. And it is Queequeg's coffin that aptly at the end saves Ishmael to record their idyll as an essential of the greater epic. It has been rightly pointed out that here is one of the great interracial friendships of American literature, along with Natty Bumpo and Chingachgook, Huck Finn and Jim.

Queequeg represents one other aspect of the human microcosm: the innocent belief that the individual will is utterly free, almost untrammeled even by circumstance, with the area of environmental conditioning and influence held to be immeasurably less than by civilized thinkers. It is, however, finally not his will to live until he returns to his people that conquers the illness to whose fatality he is at first resigned; he dies after all without realizing his intention. His all-will is as erroneous in Ishmael's eyes as Stubb's all-fate.

★ FLASK

There is a reason Ahab divides the world between Starbuck and Stubb, omitting Flask. Flask's prowess is not the courage wrested from respect for fear; it is the rash heedlessness of youth and unconcern. His devil-may-care is a natural, Stubb's a deliberate, attitude. Flask's unconcern stems from a mind that mirrors the mediocrity of most, without the saving grace of goodness in the many. He is the materialist without a shred of taste or graciousness to temper his gross appetites.

His cruelty is not deliberate; it is the natural ferocity of the wild. He is not so much moral or immoral as amoral, too much the animal to have a sense of freedom and its consequent responsibility. Yet he faces the end fearlessly, characteristically mixing thoughts of money and mother, the only mention granted his human attachments.

★ PIP

In his first appearance Pip cringes in fear as a storm strikes. His cowardice might have remained forever passive, except that a substitute was needed in Stubb's boat. Once, twice Pip jumps from the boat, the first time to be saved by cutting the line and losing the whale, the second time left to be picked up by the ship itself. He drowns in reason, if not in fact, thereafter harping endlessly on the tune of Pip the coward having disappeared, in mental dissociation from the guilty act.

His lament of cowardice is an ever-present reminder to Starbuck, Stubb and crew of their own lack of courage in the face of Ahab. To Ahab he is a reminder of Ahab's own madness which dissociates him (Ahab) from his own boy. Ahab takes Pip into his cabin; but once on The Line, Ahab finds his appeals to give up the white whale too tender and so commands Pip to stay in the cabin from which Ahab then keeps himself. So Ahab severs almost his final human tie, his symbolically adopted son. Pip, staunchly obedient to the command, goes down in the ship without ever seeking refuge on the deck, thus erasing the stain of his earlier guilt. He becomes then (a parallel to the Pilot Boy in "The Ancient Mariner") illustration that the innocent too must suffer, even die, because of the sins of others.

★ CREW

In the whaling industry, even more than on the American frontier, one could find a ready microcosm of human kind in religion, race and nationality. The crew of the *Pequod* forms such a microcosm. It evidences therefore a natural democracy of ability and achievement in their chosen pursuit—whaling. Doubtless the captains and higher mates (captains in training) would always be whites close to the owners, but beyond that all had every opportunity of rank and "lay." Even the ideal "community" erupts with racial prejudice, however, as the Spanish sailor, raising the Moorish past, taunts Daggoo with his blackness. Only the crashing storm forestalls a near riot. Only a night's diversion could give rise to what the life-and-death business of actual whaling would hardly permit.

Thirty-eight seamen are identified, not counting those in Ahab's phantom crew aside from Fedallah. Most are given some individual status in the microcosm. Bulkington is the steadfast helmsman. Perth, the Blacksmith, exemplifies those who go whaling to escape from lives become impossible on land. The Carpenter is as stolid as the material of his craft. The old Manxman serves as proverbial oracle who sounds much wiser than he is. The steward's tolerance of Stubb's idea of a joke seems stronger than Stubb's own. Daggoo is instanced as perfect coordination, poised upright in the whaleboat with Flask atop his shoulders. Tashtego remains almost unaffected by man and circumstance, favoring or adverse.

All of the crew perish with Ahab, for all (like the crew in "The Ancient Mariner") are variously involved in the collective guilt, whether from greed (money), demonic bent, love of the chase, or fear. And the innocent are as subject to natural terror and catastrophe.

★ AHAB

Ahab is a big man: physically, mentally, spiritually. His hunting prowess is long established and still apparent in his middle age. His mental stature is laid bare in his soliloquies. Spiritually, he moves among universals, challenging God

Himself in the name of the Devil and accepting the eternal consequences. Once giant Ahab takes over the stage, his human cohorts pale beside him. Hence the detailed introduction establishing Ishmael as both youthful experiencer and matured, articulate narrator—to insure reader acceptance of his point of view.

Ahab's story does not begin with the loss of his limb to Moby-Dick. He himself laments to Starbuck "the madness, the frenzy, the boiling blood and the smoking brow, with which, for a thousand lowerings old Ahab has furiously, foamingly chased his prey—more a demon than a man!" The continuity was hardly interrupted by a day's honeymoon with "the young girl-wife" he took at fifty. Was it the cumulative loss of living no less than the climax-capping loss of limb to Moby-Dick that drove him to rage against the rage of the chase within him, to avenge the final hurt he could not fathom in self or circumstance? What begins, ostensibly, as vengeance upon a creature becomes defiance of all the universal inscrutability, arbitrariness, injustice and malevolence that creature represents to him.

From first to last Ahab is hopelessly split and torn: between thought and feeling; between sanity and madness; between his remorseless will and predetermined fate; between Christian obedience and satanic defiance; between good and evil as warring entities; between seeing incidents as deterrents and as spurrings; between longed-for release from conflict, like Pip, and resolve to ride out all irresolution.

Precisely his ascendancy over the irresolvable conflict and his humor at his own expense save him from monsterdom and utter madness; make him Satanically heroic, and yet angelically lost; transform his end into a kind of crucifixion for all who rail at the universal whim, but are not nerved to opposition. The more he says his quest is fated, the more he makes it so. The more he reasons about his impotence in madness, the more he asserts the power of his will. Thus at the end, trapped, he yet acts as though he is a free agent and knowingly accepts the consequences of his freedom to act. Flaunting, ridiculing, misinterpreting, defying God, he never loses faith in Him. We remind ourselves that this is how the older meditative Ishmael sees Ahab and his hunt. We must accept his view in fiction, whether or not in fact.

Ahab's tradition, immediate and remote, is Christian; its kelson is the command to "love the Lord thy God with all thy heart and thy neighbor as thyself." Ahab's hatred of God forces renunciation of his love for his fellow men—his employers, his crew and their families, the sons of the *Rachel,* Pip, his own wife and son—each a further cut in a deepening anguish. As he says, "Ahab stands alone among the millions of the peopled earth, nor gods nor men his neighbors!"

One can say, finally, Ahab becomes so intent on his own final sacrifice upon the altar of defiance that he abandons every caution. Had he remained quite cool he might well have won out over an already wounded whale carrying several harpoons, entangling lines and a human corpse. Ahab overreaches himself every bit as much as he is set down by the forces that oppose him. How ironically right is his own "It is true worship to will to be one's self."

★ FEDALLAH

"Ahab's shadow" seems sometimes like a shadow's shadow, so hardly human does one find him. He serves as Ahab's alter ego, prophesying their joint demise. The start of their association no one knows. Ahab must have been Fedallah's quondam convert to the Parsee faith (note that Elijah speaks of Ahab's battling before a Spanish altar, sure sign of some apostasy). Convert becomes more faithful than his teacher: Ahab calls down the powers of the darker side and hurls defiance at the very gods; Fedallah shudders in terror and wears the ashen face of death.

More symbol than man, Fedallah represents that heresy in Ishmael's universe (Parsee, Manichean, or what not) which divides God's unity into distinct forces of good and evil. Ahab does not divide the universe so much as he divides himself. He defies the Christian god instead of deserting him, and defies as well the Parsee fire instead of fatalistically accepting it. Ahab is victim of the contradiction, while Ishmael, in Fedallah's place, survives to reinstate the wholeness.

★ MOBY-DICK

An old, sly, big catfish in the local lake turns into larger myth, as all escapes by all the "big ones" become attributed to him. So with Mocha, or Moby-Dick: the actuality—unique in color, size, and shape—becomes the myth.

As myth he is already far more a symbol than mammalian fish. Small wonder that all who look into the mirror of the myth seem to see projections of themselves (cf. the doubloon nailed to the mast). Tashtego sees an outsize whale. Flask sees more barrels and more coin. Stubb sees in his pursuit a more than usually jolly game. Starbuck sees him as dire disaster Ahab-brought. Ishmael sees him as terror of the deep, but part of the universal whole, essentially good. Ahab focalizes in him all his regret for forty years of crazy butchery and the malevolence of a universe that permits such an unaccountable thing to happen.

Moby-Dick himself is a whale—outsize, dazzling in hue, graceful, swift and powerful beyond most, if not all. He is a formidable beast and adversary indeed, of whom one could well ask with Blake ("The Tiger") "Did He who make the Lamb, make Thee?" Yet ordinarily, he is doing what comes naturally, being a whale. He spouts, he sports, and doubtless mates; and when he is attacked he sounds, he butts, he whips his tail. Handling him becomes unpredictable when one attacks unorthodoxly—into the wind, from the front. Moby-Dick's chances of success, already good because of much prior practice, become exceptional when the hunter disowns his only advantage in the "terrain" of the whale, his reason.

★ WHALES

The typing and individualization so apparent in members of the *Pequod* crew extend to the other side of the epic conflict, the whales.

Some whales appear for typing only. Thus the "Cetology" classifies whales, but hardly in routine fashion. At one level there is the scientific classification from observation; at a second, the impressionistic one by temperament and behavior; finally, the labeling by kinds of books. The intent becomes apparent: whales in their ways are much like people in theirs, which is not to say the two are alike. Both are beings of a purposeful universe of which intelligence is the all-encompassing center. The physical ever completes itself in the spiritual; the spiritual always demands a physical embodiment.

Sea is sometimes imaged in terms of land, prairies for instance. Skies are seas and stars are sand. Natural phenomena are constantly given supranatural connotations. Humans show animal traits. Sharks, squid, brit, all serve their purposes within the grander pattern. All are in harmony despite the savage conflict, the killing and devouring of one kind by another, the destructiveness of wind, wave and will—all the raw terror is yet leashed to some inscrutable universal intent that is more good than evil.

The whale is stripped down, chapter by chapter, from blubber to bare skeleton, highlighting how fearfully and wonderfully each thing is made, and made to serve. The entire sea, in fact the universe, comprises innumerable contraries and contradictories that are yet wholly complementary.

Particular whales pursued are individuals—sick, old, sleek, ungainly, playful, pugnacious, sexual—and Moby-Dick the epitome.

A Critical Sampler

. . . If we had as much of Hamlet or Macbeth as Mr. Melville gives us of Ahab, we should be tired even of their sublime company. Yet Captain Ahab is a striking conception, firmly planted on the wild deck of the *Pequod*—a dark disturbed soul arraying itself with every ingenuity of material resources for a conflict as once natural and supernatural in his eye, with the most dangerous extant physical monster of the earth . . .

Evert Duyckinck in *The Literary World,* IX
(November 22, 1851), 404

Not only is there an immense amount of reliable information here before us; the *dramatis personae,* mates, harpooners, carpenters, and cooks, are all vivid sketches done in the author's best style. What they do, and how they look, is brought to one's perception with wondrous elaborateness of detail; and yet this minuteness does not spoil the broad outline of each. It is only when Mr. Melville puts words into the mouths of these living and moving beings, that his cunning fails him, and the illusion passes away. From the Captain to the Cabin-boy, not a soul amongst them talks pure seamen's lingo . . .

Albion, n.s. X (November 22, 1851), 561

. . . It is a canon with some critics that nothing should be introduced into a novel which it is physically impossible for the author to have known.

Spectator, XXIV (October 25, 1851), 1026

. . . For, in sober truth Mr. Melville's vanity is immeasurable. He will either be first among the book-making tribe, or he will be nowhere. He will centre all attention upon himself, or he will abandon the field of literature at once. From this morbid self-esteem, coupled with a most unbounded love of notoriety, spring all Mr. Melville's efforts, all his rhetorical contortions, all his declamatory abuse of society, all his inflated sentiment, and all his insinuating licentiousness.

The Democratic Review, XXX
(January, 1852), 93

. . . All the rules which have been hitherto understood to regulate the composition of works of fiction are despised and set at naught. Of narrative, properly so called, there is little or none; of love, or sentiment, or tenderness of any sort, there is not a particle whatever; and yet, with all these glaring defects, it would be in vain to deny that the work has interest.

Dublin University Magazine, XXXIX
(February, 1852), 223

Melville was anatomizing his own soul: his contempt for the herd, his No-saying, in thunder. The monomania of Ahab was his own. There is no blasphemer like a Puritan backslider, but such renegade blasphemy is always accompanied by brooding moroseness and secret horror leading often to insanity . . .

Frederick Lewis Pattee in *The New American Literature 1890-1930.* New York: The Century Co., 1930, 379

In his "human" self, Melville is almost dead. That is, he hardly reacts to human contacts any more: or only ideally: or just for a moment. His human-emotional self is almost played out. He is abstract, self-analytical and abstracted. And he is more spell-bound by the strange slidings and collidings of Matter than by the things men do . . .

D. H. Lawrence in *Studies in Classic American Literature.* New York: The Viking Press, Inc., 1951, 158

. . . The skill of these preparatory passages can be too readily overlooked, either in irritation at their superficial incongruity or in impatience at the continued delay of the start of the whaling-voyage proper; but unless it is remarked and remembered how the vision of the great central symbol of the book is first hinted at, then reiterated in countless small details (like the pictures on the inn-walls, the implements of the chase, and the very names of the taverns themselves), as well as in constant oblique references to the whale itself, and finally expanded and elaborated in the great set piece of rhetoric in Chapter IX, the unusually subtle and effective marshalling of the two principal contestants for the conflict that begins with the sailing of the *Pequod* will not be fully appreciated . . .

Ronald Mason in *The Spirit Above the Dust,* London: John Lehmann, 1951, 117

The community of all genuine primitivists in the recent history of Western art may be visualized through a metaphoric use of one of Melville's scenes in *Moby-Dick.* In the sixty-first chapter Stubb kills a sperm whale. Ishmael's account proposes once again that sacramental acts engage the imagination of the artist. For Stubb is later to eat of the body of that whale, and Ishmael is to exclaim: "That mortal man should feed upon the creature that feeds his lamp, and, like Stubb, eat him by his own light" (Ch. LXV) . . .

James Baird in *Ishmael.* Baltimore: Johns Hopkins Press, 1956, 337

It is not contention that Melville was deliberately trying to approximate Shakespeare's different levels of providing the story of whaling for the groundlings, and the study of Ahab's sense of evil, together with the metaphysical scrutiny of 'The Whiteness of the Whale,' for those who could follow him. But so far as we can trace the genesis of any creative process, we have an example here of how Melville's own sense of life had been so profoundly stirred by Shakespeare's that he was subconsciously impelled to emulation . . .

F. O. Matthiesen in *American Renaissance.*
New York: Oxford University Press, 1941, 415-416

The logic of Moby-Dick's appearance at this moment is perfect. So long as some light of faith remained in Ahab's mind, Moby-Dick remained elusive. Recently, when the light was burning very low, Moby-Dick had been reported. And now, the wrong choice having been made calmly and deliberately, that monstrous apparition of evil turns up immediately, right under Ahab's nose. This eventuality became inevitable—almost—when Ahab broke the quadrant . . .

M. O. Percival in *A Reading of Moby-Dick.*
Chicago: The University of Chicago Press,
1950, 110. Copyright 1950 by the University of Chicago.

Within and beyond the blocks of comedy with which he paced his novel, Melville used humor as an oblique approach to the tragic and metaphysical meanings of his story. Many of *Moby-Dick's* narrative and philosophical themes are first stated—sometimes solely stated—in comic terms. The method by which this is accomplished is usually Melville's characteristic analogical or contrapuntal technique: the juxtaposition of fact and symbol. It is the ambiguous effect of humor in such passages at once to link the two planes of meaning and to obscure the connection between them . . .

Edward H. Rosenberry, *Melville and the Comic Spirit.* Cambridge, Mass.: Harvard University Press, 1955, 134

The style of *Moby-Dick* is a rhythm of three basic styles: the style of fact, the style of oratorical celebration of fact, the style of meditation moving toward mysticism . . .

Richard Chase in *Herman Melville: A Critical Study*. New York: The Macmillan Company, 1949, 91-92

Selective Bibliography: Melville and *Moby-Dick*

1. BIBLIOGRAPHY

Stern, Milton R. *The Fine Hammered Steel of Herman Melville*. Urbana: University of Illinois Press, 1957.

Stovall, Floyd (ed.). *Eight American Authors: A Review of Research and Criticism*. New York: The Modern Language Association of America, 1956 (Melville section by Stanley T. Williams).

Thorp, Willard. *Herman Melville*. New York: American Book Company, 1938.

2. TEXT

The Works of Herman Melville. Standard Edition 16 vols. London: Constable and Company, 1922-4.

Davis, Merrell R., and Gilman, William H. (eds). *The Letters of Herman Melville*. New Haven: Yale University Press, 1960.

Hutchinson, W. M. "A Definitive Edition of *Moby-Dick*," *American Literature*, XXV (January 1954), 472-78.

Mansfield, L. S., and Vincent, H. P. (eds). *Moby-Dick*. New York: Hendricks House, 1952.

Metcalf, Eleanor M. (ed.). *Journal of a Visit to London and the Continent by Herman Melville 1849-1850*. Cambridge, Mass.: Harvard University Press, 1948.

Thorp, Willard (ed.). *Moby-Dick*. New York: Oxford University Press, 1947.

3. BIOGRAPHY

Anderson, C. R. *Melville in the South Seas.* New York: Columbia University Press, in cooperation with Modern Language Association of America, 1939.

Arvin, Newton. *Herman Melville.* New York: William Sloane Associates Inc., 1950.

Gilman, William. *Melville's Early Life and Redburn.* New York: New York University Press, 1951.

Howard, Leon. *Herman Melville.* Berkeley and Los Angeles: University of California Press, 1951.

Leyda, Jay. *The Melville Log: A Documentary Life of Herman Melville, 1819-1891,* 2 vols. New York: Harcourt, Brace, and Company, 1951.

Metcalf, Eleanor M. *Herman Melville: Cycle and Epicycle.* Cambridge, Mass.: Harvard University Press, 1953.

Mumford, Lewis. *Herman Melville.* New York: The Literary Guild of America, 1929.

Sealts, M. M. *Melville's Reading, A Check-List of Books Owned and Borrowed.* Cambridge, Mass.: Harvard University Press, 1950.

Weaver, Raymond M., *Herman Melville, Mariner and Mystic.* New York: George H. Doran Co., 1921.

4. CRITICISM

Baird, James R. *Ishmael.* Baltimore: The Johns Hopkins Press, 1956.

Blackmur, R. P. *The Expense of Greatness.* Gloucester, Mass.: Peter Smith, 1940.

Bowen, Merlin. *Long Encounter: Self and Expression in the Writings of Herman Melville.* Chicago: University of Chicago Press, 1960.

Braswell, William. *Melville's Religious Thought.* Durham: Duke University Press, 1943.

Brooks, Van Wyck. *The Times of Melville and Whitman.* New York: E. P. Dutton, 1947.

Chase, Richard. *Herman Melville, A Critical Study.* New York: The Macmillan Company, 1949.

Geist, Stanley. *Herman Melville, the Tragic Vision and the Heroic Ideal.* Cambridge, Mass.: Harvard University Press, 1939.

Hetherington, Hugh W. *Melville's Reviews: British and American, 1846-1891.* Chapel Hill: University of North Carolina Press, 1961.

Hillway, Tyrus, and Mansfield, Luther S. (eds). *Moby-Dick Centennial Essays.* Edited for the Melville Society. Dallas: Southern Methodist University Press, 1953.

Levin, Harry. *The Power of Blackness.* New York: Alfred Knopf, 1958.

Mason, Ronald. *The Spirit above the Dust: A Study of Herman Melville.* London: John Lehmann, 1951.

Matthiessen, F. O. *American Renaissance.* New York: Oxford University Press, 1941.

Mayoux, Jean-Jaques. *Melville.* Evergreen Profile Book. New York: Grove Press, Inc., 1960.

Olson, Charles. *Call Me Ishmael.* New York: Reynal & Hitchcock, 1947.

Percival, M. O. *A Reading of Moby-Dick.* Chicago: The University of Chicago Press, 1950.

Rosenberry, E. H. *Melville and the Comic Spirit.* Cambridge, Mass.: Harvard University Press, 1955.

Sedgwick, William E. *Herman Melville: The Tragedy of Mind.* Cambridge, Mass.: Harvard University Press, 1944.

Spiller, R. et al. (eds). *A Literary History of the United States.* New York: Macmillan Co., 1948.

Stern, Milton R. *The Fine Hammered Steel of Herman Melville.* Urbana: University of Illinois Press, 1957.

Stone, Geoffrey. *Melville.* New York: Sheed & Ward, 1949.

Thompson, Lawrance. *Melville's Quarrel with God.* Princeton: Princeton University Press, 1952.

Thorp, Willard. *Herman Melville.* New York: American Book Company, 1938.

Vincent, Howard P. *The Trying Out of Moby-Dick.* Boston: Houghton Mifflin Company, 1949.

Wright, Nathalia. *Melville's Use of the Bible.* Durham: Duke University Press, 1949.